AF427101

Forbidden

Brianna Pitstick

A Memoir

Paperback ISBN 979-8-218-16652-6

First printing 2023

Chapter One

There's a hush that blankets the world just before morning. That instant where the bonds of sleep are struggling to keep hold but consciousness is intent on pulling back the veil. There was always a faint sense of finality when I open my eyes. Sometimes it verges on dread and other times it more closely resembles grim acceptance. Today was a grim acceptance sort of day. I lay in bed, allowing myself a few minutes to enjoy the dark quiet of my bedroom and hoping the weight against my chest would let up enough so that I could draw a proper breath.

I had a complicated relationship with silence. It was something to both treasure and fear. Silence was my sons sleeping peacefully in the mornings but it was also disapproving looks and rolled eyes. Silence was angry tension that you could cut with a knife and a swallowed sense of shame. Silence was a parade of thoughts unsaid and buried deep. For now, silence was a moment to myself where the world held still just long enough for me to catch my breath before I ever got the chance to lose it. Unable to help myself, I glanced over to look at my husband, Chris. Annoyingly, he was taking up the majority of the bed yet again; at some point he'd commandeered all of the blankets and now his body was drenched in shadow, the gentle rise and fall of his breathing a familiar accoutrement to the creaks and groans of our home.

Rather than connection, the broad expanse of his back sent a chill through me. Being able to lie next to someone and still ache with loneliness had to be a superpower of some kind; one that I seemed to have in spades. I wondered sometimes if this inability to truly connect made me the hero or the villain. The way that Chris looked at me sometimes said clearly that it was the former rather than the latter. I lifted a hand, pressed my fingertips against his bare skin, and tried to feel something. Anything that would ease the chasm whispering for sustenance just beneath my breastbone. This was my husband, the man I shared everything with, the man I'd been in love with since I was eighteen. There should have been something there. Instead, I may as well have been touching a stranger.

Chris shifted, grumbling in his sleep, and I shied away and sat up. I'd lingered long enough. It was time to get up and get things started. The kids I babysit for would be here soon, and not long after that my own kids would be waking up to start their morning. Everyone would need breakfast and clean clothes to wear. *'When was the last time I washed Liam's Batman shirt?'* I mused, slipping out of bed and padding barefoot towards the bathroom. *'Matt needs to practice going to the potty today. He got out of it all yesterday because I was busy, but at this rate he won't be ready to start preschool next year. Oh, and I need to do something about the hallway bathroom. It's basically a biohazard. Did I take anything out of the freezer last night for dinner?'*

It all seemed never-ending. But that was the easy part, letting the long litany of obligations I had piling up on my plate take over my thoughts and overshadow everything else. No one ever felt empty inside while making peanut butter and jelly sandwiches or picking up Legos. It was one of the perks of having children;

somehow, they always managed to put things into perspective. Or, in my case, blur the perspective long enough to help me get through the day without crying. Something I seemed to be doing a lot more often these days. I got dressed, pulling on an old pair of jeans and a T-shirt, and brushed my hair and teeth. I was contemplating makeup with zero enthusiasm when I happened to catch my reflection's gaze.

There were bags beneath my eyes.

Bags so deep they might as well have been designer. I ran my hands across my face and turned away rather than stare at myself for too long. I knew what I would find if I did, and it scared me. My expression was worn, tired in a way that went beyond lack of sleep and hinted at something broken and vulnerable. It wasn't a part of myself I cared to explore, not with Chris in the other room. He'd be up soon and I didn't want to have to explain something I didn't fully understand for myself.

Instead, I checked my cell. Sure enough there was a message waiting. I babysat for a little extra money a few days out of the week. Usually the kids got here fairly early so that their moms could get to work. Since I didn't want to wake anyone in the house, they let me know via text when they were on their way so that I could meet them at the front door. I trooped downstairs and settled by the living room window to wait. A few minutes later, headlights danced across the wall and ceiling and I opened the door just as my client climbed out of her car with her children. I took the little girl, Emily, and carried her back to bed to sleep for a while longer before the rest of the house rose for the day. My second protégé, a baby less than six months old, was soon settled as well. I liked sitting with him in the living room while he dozed off to sleep.

I'd always been a nurturer. It was something that came naturally and once I became a mother, I did everything that I could to cultivate that part of myself. It was fulfilling…to an extent at least. Once the baby was asleep, I peeked in on my two youngest to find them still blissfully unaware. I passed my eldest in the hall as he wandered towards the living room. He was still half-asleep and kindergarten didn't start for a few more hours but a little exhaustion wasn't about to keep him from morning cartoons. As I moved around the house, setting out toys and coloring books in preparation for the younger kids, I tried to stay as quiet as possible. Chris complained about how noisy we all were in the mornings and I did what I could to let everyone sleep undisturbed for as long as possible. Eggs and pancakes were a good way to spend my free time as the kids began to wake up. I wasn't much of a cook but even I could admit that the scent of breakfast was more than a little enticing.

Having a full house might have been intimidating to some, but for me it was just like any other day. The silence was precious, especially with so many people at the house. The only other time it was ever this quiet was at night after the boys were finally coerced into bed. A sound caught my attention and I turned in time to see the garage door close. I shook my head. Chris was awake and going about his morning routine. He'd smoke for a few minutes and come back in smelling like stale cigarettes and coughing with every breath. He knew that I knew he smoked, but he didn't seem inclined to stop and didn't care enough to hide it from me.

It was almost 7:00 am and Chris would be leaving soon. The urge to kiss him or hug him before he walked out of the door assailed me. Anything to reconnect even for a few seconds. I wanted to do something to alleviate this pressure in my chest, but didn't have the time and wasn't sure he would welcome the affection or question my motives. I sighed and darted back to the refrigerator. Everyone had different taste buds and it was a challenge in itself trying to prepare a breakfast that wouldn't offend any of them. I'd already fed the baby but already he was starting to fuss again, so I paused long enough to check on him before rushing back to finish fixing plates. The dishes were already beginning to pile up but I wouldn't be able to get to them until later. Emily was starting to show signs of autism and between cleaning up thrown food and calming her frequent tantrums, I would have my hands more full than usual.

My shoulders threatened to sag but I forced myself to straighten. Just thinking about what awaited me was enough to drain what little energy I had. Sometimes I barely had enough energy to take a shower let alone juggle a house full of small children, run our household, and cater to my own husband. This wasn't how I'd pictured my life turning out, and yet again restlessness stirred in my blood. I loved my family, but sometimes the sense of being trapped in a cage was too overpowering to ignore. Tears pricked my eyes but I ignored them, instead focusing on straightening up the kitchen and putting away bowls while the kids migrated towards the living room to immerse themselves in morning cartoons.

Chris was already gone. At some point he'd come back in from the garage only to turn around and leave again. Not once did he acknowledge me or even meet my eyes beforehand, and a bolt of hurt shot through me. It was hard to remember what things had been like in the beginning. When our relationship had still been fresh and new, when the world had been full of possibility and wonder. We'd spent hours talking about our future together; our hopes and dreams. I wanted to believe that the couple we'd been, the kids who'd been so confident that things would fall into place, were still there deep down but I didn't know how to find them.

I remembered the first time I met him and the way he'd brought stability and purpose to my life. My previous boyfriend had been an emotionally abusive lush. I'd been convinced that I could fix him; I didn't of course, but he wasn't the first boy I'd gravitated towards because of some internalized desire to take care of them. I'd always wanted to feel needed and these days, that translated into an at-home daycare center. Which was infinitely healthier than playing 'build-a-boy' with an emotionally damaged lover.

By comparison, Chris seemed to have his shit together. He made me feel wanted, needed, important. For a girl who was used to being summarily ignored, it was kind of a big deal. I was always 'one of the guys,' the best friend and confidant. Growing up the idea of stability – the idea that I could belong – had always been a wild concept just out of my reach. My mother died when I was still young and her love affair with the bottle had been a source of contention between her and my dad. My sister and I were already living with our dad when she died.

My sister and I had only been able to see her on the weekends when she was alive and her passing was devastating for more than one reason. Our time together had been cut short yet again, and the sense that there had been things left unsaid between the two of us still haunted me. It didn't help that at the time, I was still struggling to fit in with my new family, despite having lived with them for over a year. It always felt as if I needed to prove that I was just as good as my stepsiblings, that I belonged.

Unfortunately, I always ended up feeling defective and inadequate. It was impossible not to feel out of place, especially since my dad was a man of few words when it came to things like emotion. By senior year, I'd managed to convince my dad to help me get an apartment of my own. My parents refused to let me back into the house after a particularly heated argument one day. I came home to find all of my clothes in a garbage bag outside. Since I had to go to work that day, I didn't have time to force the issue. I went on to live with my grandmother for a few months and after that I stayed with my sister. Finally getting a place of my own was a relief. Even so, I was adrift, without ally, but I tried to convince myself that I was grown enough not to care.

I met Zachary a year or so before graduation. He was my high school counselor, and a welcome distraction from my isolation. While I had friends in high school, I didn't have someone that I could lean on emotionally about all the things going on in my life. My journalism teacher, who was a major confidant of mine, was the one who suggested that I start going to see Zach in the first place. My home life was no secret and for those who knew where to look, it was obvious that I had a lot on my shoulders. Zachary quickly became my saving grace and his office was my sanctuary on more than one occasion. He liked being thought of as the 'cool' teacher and he was often and talking to him about all the problems I was facing at home kept me from crumbling beneath the weight of all the things I couldn't change or fix.

After high school, Chris became my rock. Being with him had been like setting anchor for the first time. With him there was a chance for a family; the kind of family I'd never truly had before. I promised myself that I would do things differently. My parents weren't bad people. Like everyone else, they did the best that they knew how. My mom especially has always been cast in an unforgiving light because of her alcoholism but she was so much more than her addiction. She was kind, she was nurturing and gentle, and – most importantly – she loved my sister and me. She was taken from me so early that I didn't get the chance to try and help her. She used alcohol to soothe those vulnerable, broken parts of herself and I'd always wished there had been something I could have done for her.

I never got the chance to help her, and I sometimes wondered if that contributed to my desire to save everyone I came across even if it meant getting hurt in the process. With Chris, for the first time, *I* was the one being taken care of. I allowed myself to be vulnerable with him, to trust that he would be there to catch me if I stumbled and fell. The freedom that having a partner offered was beyond liberating and the two of us grew closer with every passing day.

Once I realized that I was in love, things should have been simple. First comes love, then comes marriage, and then comes a baby, a house, and mortgage payments. I didn't exactly stick to the script but I'd gotten the gist of it right. It's just that, life had a way of moving much too quickly; one day the feelings I'd thought had been immortalized in the exchange of rings had faded into obscurity. When was the last time Chris looked me in the eye? When was the last time he even cared enough to be in my presence? He was always either watching television or binging on junk late at night – I knew because it was my responsibility to clean up the mess come morning since he refused to do it for himself.

We were supposed to be *that* couple. The perfect ones living behind the picket fence. But somewhere along the line we'd gotten lost and I, at least, couldn't seem to find my way back. Meanwhile,

Chris seemed oblivious that there was anything out of the ordinary and complaining about the problems I felt were obvious oftentimes left me feeling like a madwoman. Was I just the only one who saw it? Or was I the only one who cared? I couldn't tell the difference anymore.

I stopped folding laundry long enough to check the time. Almost noon. Kindergartners had half days and I was about to go from five kids to four. I gathered everyone together, making sure that they all had on shoes before herding them out to the car. The empty space where my husband's car should have been stuck out like a sore thumb. Chris didn't have a driver's license because he'd never bothered to get it renewed. Since his license had been revoked, he'd have to take several classes, pay a few hundred dollars in fines, and retake his driver's test before he was legal again. I knew it was a pain in the ass but it had been years and he never seemed to care enough to make his license a priority. Though that didn't stop him from driving himself anywhere and everywhere he wanted to go.

While my husband may have been content to get behind the wheel of a car without a valid license, I was never comfortable with it, and it irritated me to no end that he wouldn't at least put forth the effort to fix what could potentially be a huge liability for the both of us. But, like most of my concerns, Chris ignored my complaints even while I did my best to shoulder the bulk of the responsibilities. I was the one who took our son to kindergarten, watched our two youngest, ran errands, and cleaned the house.

Just thinking about all the things that I had on my plate made my shoulders sag in exhaustion. When I was little, I thought that falling in love was the fun part. After all, the people on television did it all the time. Once you found the person meant for you, happily ever after was only a hop, skip, and a jump away. To lose love was always a tragedy that no one could have predicted or avoided. A result of fate or the will of the Gods.

I wasn't the type of woman men fell head over heels for, I wasn't the type of woman who knew the taste of love at first sight. While love came as easily as breathing to some, it was always escaping my grasp when I needed it the most. Most of my life had been spent trying to figure out what was wrong with me that no one wanted to accept me the way that they did other girls my age. Meeting Chris had been like a dream come true. Not only did he care about me, he treated me with kindness and respect. He listened to what I had to say and was more attentive than anyone else in my otherwise expansive circle of friends. Though I was friendly with a lot of different people and was able to fit into a variety of cliques, something about Chris made it impossible not to trust him. He knew more about me than most of the people I hung out with at the time and I often found myself opening up to him in ways that I wasn't used to doing – and haven't been able to do again since.

I was grateful for his love. So much so that I wondered now if perhaps I loved him *because* he'd loved me. Chris proposed a few months after I found out that I was pregnant. I wanted to make a point of making sure that we weren't just getting married because we were going to have a baby together. So, we waited to get married until after our eldest was a year old. It gave us enough time to figure one another out and get used to the idea of becoming a unit. Our second son came along a few years later, and my youngest followed right on his heels. Somehow, in the midst of building a happily ever after, we lost track of one another.

Now, my husband barely looked me in the eyes and when we did speak, he was usually short with me. Was there a word to describe the sinking of your stomach and the pain in your chest every time you were with someone? Was there a phrase that encapsulated how small he could shrink you with just a look?

'Did we make a mistake.'

'Does he even love me anymore?'

The thoughts that raced through my mind on a near daily basis wound me tighter and tighter. One day I would snap, like a rubber band put under too much pressure. A shout from the living room brought me out of the quagmire of my own thoughts and I shook my head, bringing myself back to the here and now. I must have zoned out again. That was happening more and more lately. I missed my husband. Which was bizarre since we lived in the same house and slept side by side. Despite that I missed that sense of companionship we'd once shared. I was as lonely with him gone as I had been this morning laying next to him in bed. Were other marriages like ours? Or was I the only one who woke up one day just in time to realize that the warmth had left my home?

Probably.

Our married friends seemed to understand what we didn't. My former next-door neighbor and current best friend Tiffany, for instance, had it all. Including a perfect husband and marriage. Before they moved across town last month, there was never any doubt that the two of them belonged together and that their marriage was just as strong behind closed doors as it was under public scrutiny. Tiffany had things together. Her home was always immaculate, she always had dinner ready and on the table by the time her husband – another friend of mine – got home in the afternoon. It would have been easy to dislike her, but we'd hit it off from the beginning. After four years she and her husband were like family, and even though she lived further away now, Tiffany and I made sure to see one another as often as possible. Most weekends, we could be found catching up over drinks while our kids ran wild and exhausted themselves just in time to put them down for bed.

Somehow, Tiffany always seemed to have time for extra projects. Not only was she the perfect housewife, she was also an avid DIYer and she was always the one organizing playdates between the kids in the neighborhood, hosting sleepovers, and attending community events. She was the kind of mom that made each day look like a walking, talking blog post. The kind of mom that made momming look easy. The kind of mom I'd always wanted to be but could never really live up to.

Maybe, if I were more like Tiffany things would be different between Chris and me.

For what felt like the thousandth time, I shoved my dark thoughts aside. Chris loved me. Just because he wasn't as attentive or as loving as he used to be didn't mean that our marriage was failing. I just needed to try a little harder, that was all. Chris seemed content with the way things were. Maybe that meant that I was blowing things out of proportion. I was clearly the only one who thought our relationship was anything less than ideal. It was all too easy to imagine his reaction if I voiced my concerns because I'd seen his disregard play out already in real time. Whenever I suggested that we needed to make a change, he would dismiss me with such ease that I was often left feeling as if *I* were the problem.

There was no point in talking to him about what was bothering me because – when all was said and done – I really had no reason to complain. He didn't beat me or call me names and despite our problems, I appreciated Chris for being such a hardworking man. We did the best we could with what we had. Living paycheck to paycheck meant that we sometimes had to get inventive about how we paid bills and when, but somehow we managed to get by. My life may not have been as perfect as Tiffany's and I may not have had everything figured out, but my family was healthy, my kids were happy, and we had a roof over our head and food on the table.

I told myself to be content with what I had. After all, 'happy wife, happy life.' The problem was that I couldn't figure out the 'happy' part of the equation. The ingredients just weren't adding up, and it was hard to determine if those feelings stemmed from my marriage or from some defect within myself. The idea of what I would find once I opened that particular can of worms was terrifying.

It was my job to keep my family together so rather than examine my own discontent too closely, I swept my concerns under the proverbial rug, plastered a smile on my face, and simply concentrated on putting one foot in front of the other.

Chapter Two

Because my days were usually spent managing a houseful of kids, I valued the time that I got to spend with my adult friends. Rachel lived closer to the city and we were scheduled to go out. In a rare show of cooperation, Chris had agreed to watch the kids. Already, I could hear him complaining about it downstairs but I ignored him in favor of getting ready. If I entertained it, he would guilt me into staying and I needed a break not just from the kids but from my own thoughts for a while.

The front door opened and Rachel called my name. Damn. I could have sworn I had a few more minutes before she got here. Granted, I should have been ready sooner but I couldn't seem to find anything to wear. Thanks to three kids and a whole lot of stress, I'd put on a few extra pounds since getting married and the styles I'd once liked no longer seemed flattering. It was always hard to find something I felt both comfortable and attractive in so I usually tried to keep it as simple as possible. It didn't help that Chris didn't seem to care, or notice, the few times I was daring enough to step outside of my comfort zone.

I could hear Rachel and Chris laughing about something and rather than linger any longer, I grabbed a pair of jeans and a sweater. Since we were going out, I spent a little extra time on my makeup and hair before seizing my purse and keys and heading to the kitchen. I turned the corner to find my husband and one of my best friends engaged in lighthearted conversation. There was always a disconnect when I saw how Chris behaved around other people. The tension in our home was usually thick enough to touch so it was impossible not to make comparisons. He used to make me laugh. I'd forgotten about that until Rachel chuckled at something he said. Chris hadn't always been short with me. Once upon a time, the two of us had talked all the time. Now we could barely string two words together.

Rachel spotted me and shook her head. Her brow was furrowed because it had taken me so long to get ready, but there was also a smile on her face. She liked to complain about how I always took forever to put myself together, but I couldn't seem to help it. "It's about time," she snorted, getting to her feet and grabbing her purse. "You ready to go?"

"Sure." I turned to Chris as a thought occurred to me. "Can you make sure that Liam goes to bed on time tonight? No watching cartoons until he falls asleep." Liam had a lot of energy, which made putting him down for the night an adventure. He rejected the idea of bedtimes as fake news and during the day his lingering exhaustion coupled with his die-hard refusal to close his eyes for a nap made for one very cranky little boy.

He rolled his eyes and leaned back on the couch. "I don't need you to tell me that," he snapped. "Believe it or not, I know how to raise my kids."

I opened my mouth to respond but stopped myself. This wasn't the time. Our petty arguments were bad enough without making a scene in front of our friends. Instead, I leaned over him and pressed a kiss to his cheek. He didn't react and Rachel and I left while he scrolled through channels in search of something to watch. I had barely slipped into the passenger seat when she blew out the breath she'd been holding.

"What the hell was that?"

My brow furrowed. "What do you mean?"

"The way he talks to you." She glanced at me as we pulled away. "That wasn't OK."

I lifted my shoulder in a shrug, hoping to brush the incident off. "It's not a big deal really." Which was true. Tonight had been mild compared to some of the other things Chris has said to me.

"That's kind of the problem."

Frowning, I studied her profile as she drove. "What do you mean?"

Rachel sighed. "He's *always* like that." Her hands tightened on the steering wheel, "Every time I see you two together, he's talking down to you like you're an idiot."

That shocked me. This was the first time someone else had confirmed something I'd long suspected. The occasional spat was one thing, but Rachel was right; it was every time we were together. When we spoke at all it lacked the care and love I saw other couples exhibit. A part of me had wanted to believe that it was all in my head. It was better than the alternative, which was that my husband didn't even respect me enough to speak to me like an adult let alone the person he'd chosen to spend the rest of his life with.

"Doesn't it bother you?"

Did it bother me? Absolutely. Some days all I could do was break down and cry. It was so bad now that the urge to cry struck me when I least expected it, coming out of the blue to steal the starch from my spine and eclipsing once sunny days. I knew the signs of depression thanks to my mom. Sadness and alcohol often went hand in hand, though she did what she could to shield me from certain truths the same way I worked to keep my boys oblivious to my growing melancholy. Hiding my feelings from the kids was hard enough without Chris always taking shots at me. Thanks to his near constant rhetoric, I dreaded the thought of going home and having to see him. I was always worried that something I said or did would be taken the wrong way and start yet another argument.

Just thinking about it now was enough to make my pulse race and my breath hitch. The idea of coming home shouldn't be enough to bring me to the brink of a full-blown panic attack, but it did. My house wasn't the sanctuary it was meant to be. At some point it had become something else. Something impossibly heavy. One day, I was afraid it would crush me.

It should be noted, of course, that I wasn't perfect.

It's easy, when arguments arise and unpleasant feelings become the norm, to lose sight of the part I played in the derailment of our marriage. It's easy to point to all the ways that Chris came up short as a partner and a husband, but I'm sure he could say the same about me. When we first started dating, I was extremely insecure thanks to my past relationships. That insecurity caused me to overact, which put a strain on us both. There was a part of me that expected Chris to understand where I was coming from and fix what was broken. When he didn't, it left me with a sense of resentment I couldn't shake, and often held against him. After our first child, I started going to a therapist on a regular basis. A mixture of therapy and maturity taught me how to deal with my emotions more effectively, but I still had a long way to go. The difference between who I was now and who I used to be is that I knew how to recognize where my weaknesses lay.

The difference between Chris and me?

I wasn't in denial of my shortcomings and I didn't try to push them off onto him. Chris liked to attribute his bad behavior to the problems we had early on. He wasn't willing to take responsibility for the ways he may have hurt me because to do so would be to admit that he wasn't infallible. The truth was that he didn't change towards me until years after I first started taking ownership of my behavior so that I could change for the better.

It was demoralizing to work on yourself, to strive to be better, only to have the person you wanted to change for use your past transgressions as permission to treat you like garbage. Chris provided for us and loved us, but was that really enough? Did it negate the moments he made me feel less than what I was worth?

I didn't know.

My stomach twisted as guilt assailed me.

'Chris is good to me,' I thought firmly. *'He can be an ass but he's a good man. It's not like he cheats on me or——'*

"Bri?"

My thoughts came to a screeching halt at the sound of Rachel's voice. What was wrong with me? It's not like any of this was news. Chris had been this way for years. By now it was something I should have been used to.

Only, I wasn't. On top of that, something about hearing someone else point it out made it more real. Made it something worth paying attention to. Forcing myself to calm, I tried to focus on what Rachel was saying but it was nearly impossible. The rest of the night passed in a blur. Over the next few weeks, my conversation with Rachel kept replaying in my mind. She'd always been protective of me, which was where her comments from the other night had likely stemmed from. Even though I was able to justify her accusations, I couldn't dismiss them entirely. Which was why, when I found myself sitting in Tiffany's garage a few months later, my eyes almost bugged out of my head when she turned to me with a frown and said:

"How are things between you and Chris?"

"Fine." I shrugged. Then, thanks in part to Rachel's reaction that night, I continued. "Why?"

She proceeded to tell me, in no uncertain terms, that she was worried. According to Tiffany, Chris hadn't been a very good husband during the last few years.

"I can tell something's up with you." She took a sip of her beer and I did the same to give myself time to respond. She was the second person to bring it up, and for the first time I started to wonder if maybe there was something truly wrong. Maybe our issues weren't just in my head. The rest of the day was spent deep in thought. When Chris came home that night, I found myself studying him in a new light.

Our routine was the same but because of my friends, I began to pay closer attention to it, to study the nuances that made up our time together. There was something…off. It took me a moment to pinpoint what was wrong because I'd grown so used to it over the years. My husband didn't talk to me. The realization hit like a slap to the face. He didn't talk *to* me, he talked *at* me. I'd never made the distinction before but now it was impossible to ignore. It was something I sometimes did with the kids because they were so young and couldn't argue back. It wasn't about communicating feelings and ideas the way that partners should with one another. Chris spoke to me as if he doubted my level of intelligence, dismissing my insight as easily as one would brush aside a gnat, only with less derision.

Rachel's words floated through my mind and I tensed. She'd been right but that didn't mean I liked to admit it. I'd known it all along, but there was just something about having other people pointing out the cracks in our marriage that made me examine our problems more closely. All this time I'd been under the impression that if I just kept my mouth shut that things would eventually get better. Or at least no one would have to know just how bad they'd become. But it was too late. The cat was out of the bag, assuming it had ever been in the bag in the first place. I wasn't the only one who knew that our 'rough patch' had somehow become a long, dead-end road. If my friends could see it, that meant that our kids might be able to as well. Growing up I'd picked up much more than the adults in my life had ever given me credit for, especially when it dealt with the dynamic of the people around me. I looked towards my parents as guides – examples on how to handle social interactions – so I noticed little discrepancies that they otherwise tried to hide, even though I had no way to comprehend or articulate exactly what I was picking up on.

Just as upsetting as the thought that our boys may notice the tension between us was the knowledge that if I didn't do or say something now, then I might never have the courage to do so. Did I really want to spend the rest of my life biting my tongue and walking on eggshells? I deserved better. More importantly, I *wanted* better. If I was ever going to get what I wanted then I would have to fight for it.

My first battle would be convincing Chris to go to therapy with me, and it wasn't until almost April that I worked up the nerve to broach the topic.

Chris was notoriously stubborn about such things, but counseling had been my saving grace. My dad wasn't callous, but he was blunt and he shied away from what he viewed as excessive displays of emotion. When my mom died, tears hadn't exactly been prohibited but they hadn't been encouraged either. That was the theme for my entire life: love, anger, fear, sadness. Emotions were something you put up with, not something you explored and unraveled. My high school counselor, Zachary, had been the first person to ever help me feel validated. Zach helped me open up and talk about the things that bothered me before they could fester and grow into something ugly. He'd been my shoulder to cry on and a sympathetic ear when things at home got hard. Sharing my thoughts and fears with someone who listened to me had been a weight off my shoulders. Zach had been more than a counselor, he'd been an ally.

If there was one thing I needed now, it was more allies.

It was hard to say why Zach was the first name I thought of. I simply remembered him as being someone who was relatable and dependable. He was laid back and easy to get along with. Instinctively I knew that Chris would respond to Zachary much better than any other counselor I might bring him to. Which wasn't saying much, but I needed to start somewhere, right?

Before I could talk myself out of it, I got onto the computer and started searching for any sign of the man who'd played such a large part in my life. Thanks to Zach, the transition from teenager to young adult wasn't nearly as traumatic as it might have been, and the sense of comfort I felt every time I stepped into his office was still something I held close to my heart. He was surprisingly easy to track down, and when my results revealed that he was still actively practicing and relatively close by, I took it as a sign. Before I could lose my nerve, I called his main office and left a message on the direct line asking to speak with him. Reaching out to him like that was a gamble but I didn't know what else to do. Chris and I needed help and I knew that he wouldn't listen to me. Zach was an older, well-established man. He was someone Chris could relate to and hopefully that would be enough to make him take what I had to say seriously. I had a feeling that I would need all the advantages I could get.

Assuming I could get Chris to agree to go in the first place.

Zachary returned my call himself and we spoke for a few minutes while I explained my situation. He agreed to see us to determine what he could do to help, and I sighed in relief. Anxiety had convinced me that he wouldn't call me back or that he'd tell me to reach out to someone else. If I were being honest, a part of me wished that he had. He would be a familiar face but it had been years since I'd sat in his office and poured out my deepest, darkest fears and insecurities. I wasn't a teenager anymore. Zachary didn't know this new, older version of me any better than I knew what kind of person he had become. His voice may still be pleasantly familiar, but that wasn't enough to erase my lingering discomfort at the idea of airing Chris's and my dirty laundry to someone I knew.

I'd just have to cross that bridge when I got to it. The important part was that Zachary had agreed. Now for the hard part.

Like my phone call to Zachary, I knew that the best way to handle my nerves was to talk to Chris before I chickened out. Despite my resolve or perhaps because of it, my heart was racing the entire day. I tried to take my mind off what I needed to do before I gave myself a heart attack but since nothing was working, I finally decided to just go for it. Like ripping off a Band-Aid, I reasoned. Chris was sitting on the couch watching television when I finally worked up the courage to broach the subject. I sat beside him, staring blankly at the screen for what felt like ages while I scrambled to find the right words. When the silence became too much to bear, I turned to him with my heart lodged in my throat.

"We need to talk."

"Now?" He frowned. Even though he was facing the television I knew that his ire was directed at me. Frustration built within my breast. Why couldn't he look at me when he spoke? It was a simple courtesy, so why couldn't he seem to extend it to me? That gesture, so cavalier in its disrespect, galvanized me.

"Yes." My voice was stronger now and his brows shot up in surprise. "Now."

This time Chris did turn to face me. I looked into his eyes and wasn't sure what to do next. What I wanted to say felt too fragile for hurled accusations and raised voices. Though I was afraid that I would break it with clumsy words and clumsy hands, I tried anyway.

"How would you feel about marriage counseling?"

His eyes narrowed. "For who? You?"

I blew out a frustrated breath. "For us, yes."

"Why?"

"Because we need help. This…" I motioned between us and realized that I was shaking my head back and forth. "Whatever this is isn't working anymore."

"Jesus, Bri, calm down." He massaged the back of his neck, and I caught the roll of his eyes that he didn't bother to hide. "Last I checked, we were doing just fine."

By the time I gathered myself enough to try again, his attention had already wandered. My second attempt was just as ineffective as my first but he was no longer uncaring. Oh no, now he was angry. Usually I avoided challenging him because confrontation got under my skin. Most of my adult life had been spent trying to outrun the type of drama that had made up my early years. In my quest to increase my emotional fluency I'd been forced to accept some hard truths about myself. Primary among them was that I still struggled when it came to setting and protecting my boundaries. It took a long time to understand that boundaries weren't just about telling someone 'no'; they were also about acknowledging what I both wanted and needed in order to be fulfilled and striving to live within that truth regardless of who was made uncomfortable by it.

The problem was that it's nearly impossible to do when you're a wife and mother. Other people were constantly pulling at me with their own wants and needs and I was expected to fulfill them without complaint. I loved my family, but my children were too young to show me the kind of consideration I needed and Chris didn't seem to care enough to try. Which was pretty much par for the course. Chris was infamous for his cavalier attitude. His license, for instance, was only the tip of the iceberg. The fact that he didn't seem to mind driving without one was bad enough, but his indifference trickled over into other, more important aspects of our life as well. While I was pregnant with our third, he went hunting in Wisconsin. Our eldest had a vicious case of the stomach flu and sick toddlers were never a walk in the park. Meanwhile our youngest was less than a year old and required the remainder of what little attention and energy I had to spare.

Chris's destination was six hours away and not even an hour into his road trip, he ran into trouble. A cop had flagged his car for whatever reason and he'd been pulled over. As soon as the officer realized that there was a problem with Chris's license, he refused to allow him back behind the wheel of a car. Which meant that he had to call me to come and pick him up. Since the officer was still there, I also had to bring another person to drive our car back home. I called several friends before finding someone who was able to come with me.

From Chris's perspective, there was no reason why I should have been so upset. I'm sure that from his perspective it must have felt as if I were simply overreacting 'as usual.' The reality was a car with a cranky baby and a nauseous three-year-old. I spent most of my time holding a bag in the backseat so that he could throw up into it as we drove. When we finally got to Chris, his friend drove his car while I followed the two of them. For a moment I actually allowed myself a surge of relief that we were on our way back home. The moment was just that, however, because a mile down the road we stopped and Chris's friend got out and came to get into the car with me and the kids.

He explained what happened but it took a few seconds to comprehend that Chris was continuing to Wisconsin as planned and that he expected us to just go back home without him. I tried to make sense of it but couldn't. The argument that followed was a nasty one. I couldn't believe that he would take the same risk yet again, that he would be willing to put me and the kids through all of that just to turn around and blithely go on his way. Both his friend and I begged him to come home, but he would hear none of it. Back then I gave in, but that wasn't a mistake I could afford to make again.

Chris had never respected therapy.

Maybe it was pride or maybe he had a hard time swallowing that there was something he wasn't an expert at, but he liked to do things for himself. If something was broken, rather than call a professional in to handle it, he would take on the job himself despite having no training or experience. Sometimes the object in question ended up in worse shape than when he started and other times he simply lost interest or patience with it and left it half-done and forgotten.

If I let him, he would only continue treating our marriage the same way. I knew that if I had any hope of shaking this growing sense of melancholy, he had to be on board. I'm not sure how much time passed as we went back and forth, but a thrill of victory shot through me when he finally threw his hands up in frustration and agreed to see Zachary.

"Fine. If it's that big of a deal."

I knew that I hadn't convinced him of anything. He was just as set in his ways as ever before, but this was a win and I decided to run with it before he changed his mind. Somewhere deep down swirled a queasy mixture of shame and embarrassment. There was also a healthy pinch of nervous anticipation that made my hands shake and butterflies dance in my stomach. I wanted – no – *needed* to be treated a certain way by the man that I loved, and I had no idea how to get through to him. Usually it was easier to let things go just to avoid a potential argument when we didn't see eye to eye. But if my conversations with first Rachel and then Tiffany had taught me anything, it was that going that route was no longer an option.

Chapter Three

When did it start?

That's a good question. One I've been searching for the answer to for a while. The truth was that I had no idea. I've been looking for something for years. What makes it so difficult to find is the fact that I have no idea what it is or what it looks like. It's more of a feeling of belonging. Of home. Something intangible and devastating in its absence. It's crazy how you can miss something down to your bones without ever having had it before.

The first blush of love convinced me that I'd found it with Chris. But it turned out to be only temporary. In fact, I'm even more bereft than before and the sensation seized me, a yawning chasm in the pit of my chest, as Chris and I drove to Zachary's office. The steering wheel was slick beneath my hands and I tucked my hair behind one ear to break the monotony of my white-knuckled grip. According to the GPS we were only a few minutes out. We were surrounded by affluent, high-end shops and restaurants. People were everywhere, walking down the sidewalks with their arms heavy with shopping bags.

It was always a jolt to leave the small neighborhood that we called home. Our split-level home was serviced by one large grocery store and two gas stations. There were a few small shops that we frequented for our other needs, but nothing extravagant. Zachary's office was in a more urbanized part of Illinois and the difference between the city and home was like night and day. It reminded me of when I used to get out more and I was briefly distracted by a surge of nostalgia.

We parked in a relatively private parking lot in the back of a building with gray siding. Once inside we looked around, unsure of which office was Zach's, so we ended up sitting on a couch near the front entrance. It was Zach who eventually led us up the narrow staircase to his door. His was one of the few businesses residing within the converted two-story house. To the left of the steps was a small, black accent chair that backdropped the door to his office. Zach's inner sanctum was clean and cozy. The cream-colored walls were a nice contrast to the two seafoam-green coaches adjacent one another. One had been stationed in front of the window overlooking the city below while the other was tucked against the back wall beneath some framed pictures and a small bookshelf.

A brown leather chair was sitting in front of the couches and a desk teeming with paperwork had been placed along the back wall.

I caught sight of a photograph, two smiling children, before the sight of Zachary distracted me. We had been friends on Facebook for years but it was still a shock to see him face-to-face after so long. It took a moment to reconcile the man in front of me with the person I'd spent so many hours with in high school. He was just beginning to show his age and I found that I liked the lines at the corners of his eyes and the occasional streaks of gray in his hair. He still had the same smile but there was a weathered quality to him that spoke of a life lived and emotions felt.

What hadn't changed was the sense of familiarity, and subconsciously I found myself relaxing in his presence. I returned his smile as he reached out to shake first my hand and then Chris's.

"I'm glad you could make it." He nodded towards one of the coaches. "Why don't the two of you have a seat and we can get started."

Just like that the nervousness was back. This was it, the moment of truth. I snuck a peek at Chris and saw that while his face was immobile, his eyes held disdain. Great. We were off to a great start so far.

"Why don't you guys tell me why you're here today."

I stiffened and beside me, Chris did the same.

"Well," he began after a moment's silence. "My wife seems to think there's something wrong with our marriage."

"I didn't say that," I said defensively. Hadn't I? Not in so many words. "I just think we have some problems that we can't fix on our own."

Zach nodded and glanced between the two of us.

"Chris, you don't agree." It wasn't a question, which was good since Chris didn't bother with a response. Instead he sat back, his lips tightening with disapproval. He'd been like this ever since he'd agreed to come to therapy. It had taken a few days to set up an appointment and the vibe in the house was worse than ever before. Chris was more irritable than usual and he was quicker to snap at me. On one hand it cemented my belief that we needed outside help, but on the other I worried that I may have made a mistake. Was it right to force Chris to do something he was so adamantly against? Just because therapy had helped me didn't mean he'd find it useful. I'd suspected that getting him to talk would be like pulling teeth, and considering his current behavior, I knew my assumption had hit the nail square on the head.

Zach mirrored Chris and sat back in his chair. "What have you been up to since graduation?"

Taken aback, Chris's shoulders eased a fraction. "Nothing much." He hedged, still suspicious. "Working mostly. Hunting when I get the chance."

Zach nodded and the two men began talking more in depth. One thing led to another and to Chris's surprise, he realized that we all shared many of the same acquaintances. The session took a somber tone when Chris admitted that he was still trying to get over the death of one of his good friends, Brady Thomson.

Zach's eyes widened. "You knew Brady?" he asked. "It's true what they say then; this is a small world after all."

According to Zach, Brady had been a friend of his as well. Zach had counseled Brady during high school. The two had been close and Zach had viewed himself as more of a friend than an advisor. So, when he'd passed a few years ago, his news had hit Zach especially hard. The conversation continued as they remembered good times they'd shared with Brady and how they'd met him, and I sat back in my seat. I could contribute little to the discussion, but I didn't mind. Mainly because I was too busy watching Chris unwind before my very eyes. It was like a magic trick, or an illusion. I knew what Zach was doing, and maybe Chris did too but he was powerless to help himself. Tuning out the conversation I tried putting myself in Chris's shoes. He must have been anticipating the worst, but despite what he might have thought, I hadn't brought him here to play the blame game. It would have been easy, but it wouldn't have solved anything. None of this was *all* of Chris's fault any more than it was all mine.

It must have been a relief to talk about something normal, even if he knew it was just a ploy to get him to relax. It was like getting a hug when you were already flinching in preparation for a slap. The two men went back and forth for a while longer, talking easily with one another about shared experiences. Zach told us a little about his kids and his practice here in Illinois while I fidgeted in my seat. He tried to get me engaged in the conversation but I was too busy waiting for the other shoe to drop. They had to stop the pretense at some point and once he opened that can of worms Chris would go from smiling and pleasant to the surly man that had first strode into the office fifteen minutes ago.

Anxious and with no choice but to wait for Zach to circle the conversation back around to the topic at hand, I mulled over his question. Why were we here today? How had we ended up here? Where had it all started? I wish I could look back and point to a specific date and time when cracks began to appear in the foundation of our relationship, but it was impossible. At first it was a harsh word. A tense silence. Then it was arguments over stupid, petty things that seemed larger than life at the time. We went from wedded bliss to something else seemingly overnight. Our marriage was a snowball on a hill, a gentle roll that soon became an avalanche as it picked up more and more bullshit along the way. It started off small and insignificant, but all too soon things were spinning out of control and we were buried beneath the weight of all we did – and didn't – say.

Why had it gone on for so long?

Well, probably because I didn't want my marriage to end up like my parents'. Neither one of them had been all that great when it came to relationships. Grinning and bearing it only worked in theory. In reality, it meant losing yourself piece by piece either in the bottom of a bottle or – in Dad's case – in the arms of my stepmother. She was the woman who had raised me, and there was a part of me that would always love her for that reason alone. Even so, that wasn't enough to make me forget about her various faults. My parents may have been good together, but even I could tell that they had their struggles at times. Even so, neither one of them would have ever considered therapy of any kind, let alone marriage counseling.

I sighed.

It may not seem like it in that moment, but maybe this was the kick we needed to get back on track. My doubts aside, Chris was here. Something that, three days ago, I would have said was impossible.

"Bri?" I glanced up. Both men were looking at me and I flushed. "Are you alright?" Lines appeared on Zach's forehead when he frowned and I shifted in my seat, painfully aware of how cold Chris was to me in comparison to the older man's warmth.

"I'm fine. Just nervous."

"About what?"

It was so easy to talk to him. With just that short exchange I was seventeen years old again and sitting across from him as I told him about all the things eating away at me. When I didn't reply right away, he gave me a smile.

"Don't worry. We aren't going to delve into anything today. I just wanted to get the chance to speak with the two of you so that we could break the ice. After today I'd like to meet with the both of you individually. From there we can schedule another session like this one where we all sit down and touch base."

Chris and I exchanged glances in a rare show of camaraderie, and I relaxed even more. I wasn't the only one out of my depth. Chris was just as clueless as I was about what to do, maybe even more so since I've at least spoken to therapists before. Thinking back, I could recall with near crystal-clear clarity how helpless I'd felt during my first session. How there was just so much weighing on me that finding a place to start seemed impossible. Real counseling is nothing like the depictions we see on television. They don't talk about how long it can take to build a rapport between patient and therapist. How hard that first confession is to make.

They also don't talk about the relief that fills you when you finally have someone to talk to, when the burden of keeping your thoughts and feelings hidden finally falls away and leaves you bare. I wanted that for Chris. Not just for my sake or the sake of our marriage, but for his. If the last few years had been hard for me, I couldn't imagine how difficult they must have been for Chris. Especially since he wasn't normally a fan of sharing his feelings, and would have had few opportunities to talk about the problems we were having with any of his friends.

Zach leaned forward, resting his elbows on his knees and interlocking his fingers as he regarded the two of us. "Tell me," he began gently. "Why do *you* believe that you're here today, and what exactly do you hope to gain by coming?"

Chris didn't respond right away but after his initial reaction, we all knew exactly where he stood on being there. To keep the silence from growing awkward, I licked my lips nervously and ventured, "We don't communicate with one another very well. Not anymore." That seemed a safe enough place to start. Chris must have agreed because he didn't deny the assessment. "Beyond that I just wish that Chris could learn to see things from my perspective. He doesn't realize how his actions and his words come across and just how much they can hurt."

Zach sat back in his seat, nodding. "That's a good place to start."

We talked for a few more minutes, Zach doing his best to get Chris to open up about where we stood in our marriage to no avail. His earlier ease had been replaced by suspicion once again and there would be no talking to him now that he'd made up his mind to keep his mouth shut. Chris was a stubborn man, which meant that once he decided to do something, he dug in his heels until he got his way. Coupled with my aversion to confrontation, it was usually easier to let things go or never bring them up at all.

"Bri?"

I glanced up at Zach, realizing that I must have looked as spaced out as I felt.

"Yes?"

"You said that you and Chris don't communicate well 'anymore.'" He lifted his shoulder in a half shrug. "I was just asking why you believe that is. From your perspective, how has your relationship changed?"

"We used to be really close." The knowledge that we weren't any longer hit home, digging a little deeper than before. Saying the words aloud made them more real, permanent in a way they hadn't been before. "Now I…I know he loves me. I just don't know if he likes me very much."

'Am I really any better?'

The question left me breathless. Did I still love Chris? Of course. I probably always would. He was the father of my children, the man I'd built my life with and around. There would always be a place in my heart with his name on it. The real question was, did I like him? That was something I wasn't so sure about anymore. The only thing I was sure of was that counseling would fix us. It would *save* us.

We had the foundations of home and they wouldn't be so easily uprooted. We just needed a little help getting back on the right foot. Once we were back on track Chris and I would be stronger than ever. Every marriage has its problems. So what if I cried myself to sleep more often than not? So what if talking about my emotions was akin to opening an old wound?

Those things would pass eventually. Things couldn't, wouldn't, be this difficult forever. Not if I truly believed in our marriage. Which I did, despite the numerous setbacks over the last several years. I believed in us and I knew that Chris must believe as well, otherwise he wouldn't have agreed to come no matter how much I pleaded with him.

Some problems seemed insurmountable until you took that first step, until you made the conscious decision to face any issues head on. It may have taken time but I was here now, ready and willing to do just that. I just needed to figure out what exactly I was doing wrong. Zach would help me do just that, and maybe in the meantime he could teach Chris a little patience and understanding. Two things I craved desperately, especially during those days when the sadness and anxiety grew so heavy that I was afraid that I'd be crushed beneath them.

There were days when I wasn't sure if my unhappiness was the result of the depression that had nipped at my heels off and on for much of my life, or if my marriage was truly falling apart. Regardless of the exact reasoning, divorce was always a concept I shied away from. If I crumbled at every bump in the road, then how would I be able to tell if Chris and I could have been together for the long haul? In the beginning, Chris had been my forever and always. When had that changed? *Why* had it changed and how was I supposed to accept the fact that it had?

The rest of our meeting with Zach passed in a blur.

By the time we stood and headed back for the door, I was physically and mentally drained. Emptied out in a way that gripped me by the bones and left me shaking as I followed Chris back to the car. Our ride home was spent in silence. Though, after the evening we'd just had, I expected nothing less.

Chapter Four

I would have been naïve to think that getting Chris to therapy would make anything better. If anything, our first session inspired some of the biggest arguments in our relationship. Talking to Zach had only made me hyper-aware of every little issue Chris and I had. The only difference between my newfound focus and the magnifying glass I'd put up to our relationship after talking to Tiffany and Rachel was that I could no longer bite my tongue. Chris had been quick to dismiss my claims in front of Zach, and deep down I was hungry to prove him wrong. To show him, any way that I could, that I wasn't just making things up.

Of course, it didn't go over well. Chris complained about me 'getting on his case' while simultaneously ignoring me each time I pointed out something he was doing that proved my emotions valid. What made it especially hard was that I could see where he was coming from. I would hate to be criticized over every little thing that I did, especially if – like Chris – I was confident that my behavior was no big deal. There were times when I tried to stop myself, when I tried to keep my mouth shut the way I always did, but spending an hour on Zach's couch, forcing myself to relay the problems I *knew* that we were having, made that nearly impossible.

I was trying.

So why couldn't he?

Or, I suppose a more appropriate question would be: Why *wouldn't* he?

Chris's overall laziness, his lack of consideration, was getting to me more than usual. Though, I tried to remind myself to be understanding whenever I picked up plates caked with old food from around the house and tucked away on his side of the bed. After all, I knew that he was tired when he came home most days. While Chris worked first shift, the physical demands of his job left him physically and mentally drained by the time he got home. It was hard to rest during his off days because it was often the only free time he had to get anything done.

Weekends were still reserved for hanging out with his friends, despite how much I could have used his help around the house and with the kids. Even as I battled with feelings of neglect and anger that he wasn't doing more, I knew that Chris had his own things to deal with. It was hard to provide for five, and between doctor's visits, school supplies, and clothes it seemed like we were always scraping the bottom of the barrel. Chris wanted more for his family, and I suspected that not being able to give us that took a toll on his self-esteem.

No matter how hard we struggled, somehow it was never enough. Hell, I'd be tempted to give up too if I were in his shoes. Though those first days after meeting with Zach made me wonder if I already had, in my own way. Financially, I helped out as much as I could but Chris was responsible for the majority of our bills. The least I could do was watch the kids and handle things at the house. But no matter how I rationalized it, I couldn't quell the suspicion that he could, and should, be helping out more. Or at the very least cleaning up after himself so that I wouldn't have to add yet another thing to worry about to my plate. Instead he sat in front of the television, only rousing enough to defend himself whenever I lost my temper and snapped at him.

Every time I blew up at him or he blew up at me, things would calm for a while until old frustrations reared their head again and the cycle repeated itself. It was no wonder we needed Zach in our lives. There was no way we'd be able to learn how to communicate effectively otherwise. As it was, I looked forward to my solo sessions with Zach. Not only to have someone to talk to about everything that was going on, but also to escape the house for a while.

How sad was it that my therapist's office was my respite from the world instead of my own home? I wasn't prepared to unpack what it was that revelation said about the state of my relationships. Instead I focused on the way my shoulders eased, how my breathing evened out by subtle degrees, the second I stepped into his office and took a seat.

"How have you been?" he queried, and smiled. I straightened a little in my seat. It would be easy to tell myself that he was happy to see me but I knew better. Zach was just being polite. A state of affairs that I was so unused to that it felt personally motivated when it absolutely wasn't.

"Not great, to be honest."

Leaning back in his seat he regarded me from beneath his brows. "Oh? How so?"

"Chris and I had another argument," I admitted finally, trying my best to ignore the nagging voice in the back of my mind that whispered that I was betraying Chris in some way. My husband didn't like to admit when he might be in over his head and he certainly didn't accept help carefully, if at all. Talking about him with Zach, knowing full well how much he would have hated being discussed this way, left a bad taste in my mouth. Sensing my hesitation, if not the reason behind it, Zach drummed his fingers on the arm of his chair and studied me until I shifted uncomfortably beneath his regard.

"Why do you think that is?"

"Excuse me?"

"Why do you think things have been difficult this week? Does he hate the idea of coming here that much?"

Without realizing it, my body relaxed and I sighed. The questions should have rankled, but I was used to Zach. Talking to him about what was on my mind had been second nature at one point and I was desperate for that easy back and forth I'd been missing with Chris.

"He seems to think that admitting any kind of fault is some sort of reflection on his authority as a man."

Zach winced. "Can't say I was much different when I was his age." he admitted easily. "Though it must be frustrating when one of you is trying to find a solution to a problem if the other won't admit to there even being a problem at all."

I made a sound in the back of my throat that was part laugh and part choking cough. "You have no idea." Shaking my head I reached for one of the pillows off the couch next to me and clutched it against my middle. Hanging on to something, even the tiny accent pillow, eased the urge to fidget where I sat. Zach's eyes tracked the movement but he didn't question it. Instead he set aside the little notebook he'd been scribbling in as we talked and regarded me levelly.

"I didn't want to say anything before but you've seemed…" He hesitated only briefly, but it was enough time for dread to settle in my middle like a piece of lead. "Unhappy."

"People don't come to marriage counseling if they're happy, Zach." He smiled and I found myself smiling back.

"If you don't want to get into it right this second, that's fine," he assured me gently. "When there are problems in a marriage it can take a heavy toll. It's enough to make anyone act differently." His gaze turned pensive and there was something about his tone that caught me off guard. We'd seen one another a handful of times over the last several weeks and the conversation was always on me. How was I feeling? How was my relationship with Chris? Has it improved? What had we argued about? Why had we argued? What were my thoughts on our progress?

It seemed to go on forever, and suddenly I craved a normal conversation with a man. The chance at some honest give-and-take. The chance to be spoken to as an equal instead of a moron. Chris talked down to me so often that he didn't have to try and make me feel stupid for me to wonder if that was what he was thinking. I'd never experienced that with Zach. Whenever I spoke to him, I knew that he actually wanted to hear what was coming out of my mouth. Not just because it was his job either, or at least I didn't believe so. I could swear that there was genuine interest, genuine warmth, in his eyes and it made me bold enough to broach a topic I would have ordinarily shied away from.

"What about you and your wife?"

I didn't expect him to respond. My question was beyond personal and considering our relationship as doctor and patient, I wouldn't have blamed him if he'd decided to change the subject. It was one thing for me to feel comfortable enough to toe that line between professional and personal, and another thing entirely for him to go along with it. I was already preparing myself for an admonishment, so my lips parted in surprise when he glanced towards the photo I'd noticed during my initial visit and blew out a long breath instead.

"Unfortunately, yes." Zach met my eyes again and I was struck by the disappointment in his gaze, the vulnerability. It was something I'd never expected from him. Not just because he was older and my therapist, but because he'd always been a symbol of unflappable strength and calm. It was disconcerting to glimpse him as more than just an authority figure.

"My wife and I have been having some problems of our own for the last few years," he explained, running a hand through his hair and leaving it disheveled. "It's been the hardest on the kids, but we've been working on a system so they can try and have as normal of a life as possible."

Curious, I studied the picture more closely. Now that I was looking for it, it was impossible not to see their resemblance to Zach. It made me think of my boys and, unbidden, I wondered how Chris and I would handle it if we ever found ourselves in a similar position. Not nearly as well, no doubt. We couldn't even reach an understanding while living in the same house.

'Maybe we'd figure something out. For the kids.'

Maybe.

More than likely we'd end up fighting for custody. For a moment I imagined my kids the way I'd been when I was young. Insecure, unsure of my place in the world, and convinced that I was a burden to the adults in my life. I blinked back tears and shoved the thoughts away. My parents hadn't tried to stay together for my sake, but at the same time I wouldn't have wanted them to. They would have been even more miserable together than they'd ever been apart. Made all the worse by the fact that I would have blamed myself for their self-imposed misery.

Chris and I weren't my parents. I had to remind myself of that over and over again. Unlike my parents, the two of us had something worth saving. We loved one another, and we just needed to remember to act like it.

"Do you still love her?" I found myself asking, still agonizing over my own thoughts. He fell silent for a long, drawn-out moment, and then shook his head.

"I don't think I'll ever stop loving her, but I'm not *in love* with her anymore." He shrugged. "It's hard because my feelings didn't change because of anything she did, necessarily. Most of our problems arose after Carol had surgery on her back." Zach's jaw tightened. "I've always valued ambition and after her surgery, Carol seemed to have lost all of hers. It didn't help that our sex life was practically nonexistent at that point as well. Small issues blew up into larger ones and…" His shoulders slumped and he shook his head. "Sometimes people just grow apart," he continued finally. "It doesn't make the way you once felt for them any less real. It just means you need to care enough about yourself to walk away when the time comes."

"How can you tell when it's time?" My fingers entangled as I twisted my hands in my lap, squeezing until my fingertips appeared bloodless. I was terrified of what he might say, breathless with the threat of it hanging between us. Zach seemed to realize that I'd tensed as if expecting a blow because he cleared his throat and got to his feet.

"That should be enough for today." His voice was gentle, an executioner granting clemency at the last moment, and I let loose the breath I'd been holding and stood. I set the pillow aside, careful to place it just so against the other cushions, and grabbed my purse. It was hard to look at him in that moment. Mainly because I was afraid of what he might see. Relief? Or disappointment? What did I want, anyway? How was I supposed to save my marriage if I wasn't even sure if it was the right thing to do or what my motivations were for doing so?

Zach was holding the door open for me, hand resting lightly on the knob as he rocked back and forth on his heels. It had become our after-session ritual. Zach would walk me to the door, we'd exchange a polite farewell, agree that I would text him my availability for our next session or that he would text me his, and then I was on my way. There was something different about today and it didn't strike me until I glanced up to say goodbye. I was momentarily struck by the expression on his face, by the way he watched me, his eyes almost like a physical touch against my skin.

Everything within me froze when he smiled.

It was over in less than a second, but the familiarity of that smile, the affection, caught my attention. "Sorry about dumping my issues on you today," he said, bringing me back to myself. "You didn't come here for that."

"No, it's fine." I shook my head and tried to laugh. "I mean, we're friends, right? I mean, we're friends on Facebook at least, so…"

I was hoping to lighten the mood but Zach didn't laugh. Instead, his hand settled on the small of my back and he smiled down at me. "You know that I'm here for you, right? Just make sure that you call me if you need anything."

His fingers lingered for just a few seconds too long and then I was out in the hall and listening to the door shut behind me. I paused on the landing, my heart racing. What the hell was that? I didn't imagine it, did I? Zach had always been kind to me, but that wasn't out of the ordinary because he was a kind man. One of the only men in my life that made me feel understood. Whenever I was with him I was a little less alone than I was before and he treated me with a courtesy that was undeniably flattering.

Those were all things that I had come to expect from Zach.

But the look in his eyes…I'd never seen it before and even now, with the memory of the warmth of his hand still lingering against the small of my back, I couldn't put a name to the emotion there. Whatever it was, it was the opposite of neutral, the opposite of professional. Zach hadn't been looking at me as if I were nothing but a patient and old friend and my heart hammered in my chest as I made my way down the steps and to my car.

I shook my head. No, that was crazy. Whatever I thought I'd seen must have been in my head, or a trick of the light. Chris and I were rarely intimate lately, and when we were, I had a hard time getting what I needed from the experience. There was always this added layer of guilt that came over me for not enjoying our sex life as much as I used to, but I just couldn't shut my mind off long enough to get lost in the moment. It was true what they said: for women sex and emotion often go hand in hand, and I was no different. The more Chris and I argued, the more he put me down, the less sexy I felt. It is hard to have an orgasm when you're too busy doubting yourself and analyzing every touch, every kiss, every look. My run-in with Zach was proof that my body was beginning to rebel. Zach was being friendly because it's his job and because he was a kind person. Anything else was just pure imagination. It had to be. Zach saw me as a patient, not a woman.

Didn't he?

'Come on, this is Zach we're talking about.'

Right. I was reading too much into this. Starting my car, I pulled out of the parking lot. My breathing was slowing and my pulse had calmed. It was a relief to be able to rationalize the strange moment, and I was finally able to soothe the last of my frazzled nerves. Zach hadn't meant anything by what had happened, assuming he'd noticed anything amiss in the first place. More than likely, he was still feeling vulnerable after discussing his wife and kids. He'd never been shy when it came to talking about his life, but this was the first time Zach had ever opened up about problems with his marriage. I understood all too well just how bare such an admittance could leave you, and I couldn't imagine what it must have taken for him to answer my questions. How hard it must have been to admit those things to me. Despite the subject matter, I couldn't help but be pleased that we'd had the talk at all. Not only did he manage to completely distract me from worrying about Chris, but knowing that he trusted me enough to open up like he had filled me with warmth.

The change of dynamic would just take some getting used to. When we first met, I'd been too young for him to confide in. Not only did I have my own shit to deal with back then, even if he'd wanted to tell me about his problems I wouldn't have been mature enough to be of much help. Now that we were equals, it only made sense that he would see me in a different light. Not to mention it wouldn't have been appropriate for a counselor to unload his personal life onto one of his students.

Still…

I found it impossible to not compare Zach and Chris with one another as I maneuvered my way through traffic. Zach with his gentle smile, and patience. He was always so aware of me; it was there in the way he listened, not as if it were his job but as if he were truly interested in what I had to say. It was in the way he looked at me when I spoke, and the way conversation between us came so easily, like second nature. What struck the biggest chord was the fact that Zach validated my emotions and experiences. Whenever Chris and I began to argue, he would always side with me. I lived for those days when I could settle into the quiet of his office and just unpack all my fear and worry, and sadness bit by bit. He even knew about my depression, which was more than could be said for Chris.

No. That's not fair to Chris.

How deep the fissures ran was something I held close to my heart, too overwhelmed to really look at it too closely. I hid my random crying jags and bouts of lethargy from my family as best I could, though Chris paid so little attention to me that I doubted he would have noticed that something was wrong. He may have spent his free time at home, but his mind was always somewhere else. I missed the days when my husband was present in the moments we spent together.

Zach listened to me the way that Chris used to, but most importantly he treated me with a degree of respect that had been missing from my marriage for years. I snorted. No wonder I'd reacted that way to his touch. My cheeks flushed. What if he'd noticed? I didn't want our next session to be awkward, though it was impossible to imagine Zach letting such a thing get to him. Maybe he'd be flattered?

I lifted my hand to my mouth only to stop short and lower it back to the wheel.

It was impossible to know what was going on with me, but there was no denying that Zach's touch had left me shaken when it shouldn't have. No matter our problems, Chris and I were still married. I had no business thinking of Zach that way just because we were going through a rough patch.

'A rough patch is days. Weeks, even. Not years.'

I ignored my inner voice and spent the rest of the drive home focusing on the road ahead rather than the reservations whispering through the halls of my mind.

Chapter Five

Convincing Chris to stay in therapy and to take it seriously was even harder than getting him to go in the first place. After my encounter with Zach, I threw myself into trying to heal things with Chris and me with renewed vigor. A small seed of self-loathing questioned if this new burst of enthusiasm was the result of guilt rather than desire, and it bothered me that I couldn't say for sure. Not that it mattered, in the end my efforts amounted to little. Chris refused to meet me halfway. According to Zach, Chris likely had issues with ADD – which would explain his disorganization and his lack of motivation. Despite his assessment of my husband – assessments which he never hesitated to share with me – even Zach seemed to be losing patience with Chris's stubborn refusal to cooperate.

Which I understood perfectly, sadly enough.

If Chris wasn't even putting forth an effort at home then there was no way in hell he was engaging in the emotional labor the sessions seemed to require. I tried to be understanding, to give him time, but I was going nowhere fast and there was no easy solution to my problem in sight.

Nothing seemed to motivate Chris, and the more I cajoled and argued, the less inclined he was to give Zach anything he could use to work with. His attitude when we were at home was even worse. Or maybe it was because I was forced to pay closer attention to it, to examine all the little ways that we had been falling apart for years. One major point of contention happened to be our sex life, and I was sure that this was the reason behind my unwelcome reaction to Zach.

I was lying in bed one night when the reality of my situation with Chris reared its head yet again. The boys were finally down for the night so the house was uncharacteristically quiet. There had been no arguments today. In fact, there had been little interaction between us at all. It's hard to argue with someone when the other person doesn't even bother to acknowledge that you exist. Some of it was just Chris, but I sensed that at least a portion of the cold shoulder was the result of our recent sessions.

It was getting harder and harder to address moments of discontent with him. I knew that it was necessary if I ever had any hope of getting Chris to first acknowledge his part in the way things were and eventually help me fix things for the better. Unfortunately, it was hard to keep that in mind when his initial, knee-jerk reaction was to lash out or ignore me. He wasn't just resistant to change inside of

Zach's office, he was digging in his heels at every chance that he got and trying to get him to budge even an inch was wearing on me in more ways than I could count.

The one exception to the rule was when we were in bed together. There, in the comforting embrace of our bed, with the dark weighing in around us, he would reach for me. My thoughts always descended into turmoil whenever his hand brushed my skin or his lips trailed over my shoulder and neck. Not from passion, but resentment. It always seemed as if Chris only ever had time for me when it came to sex.

In the beginning, we were compatible both in and out of the bedroom. I used to enjoy sex, but somewhere along the line that enjoyment shifted to dread. In my mind he was only ever kind to me or touched me when he expected the interaction to lead to sex. It was unfair and demoralizing for a number of reasons. How was it possible to be so dismissive of someone during the day only to expect that kind of level of intimacy at night? It was impossible not to feel as if I were being taken advantage of every time we had sex and, if anything, that only compounded my rapidly growing resentment.

Before our moment in his office, I would bring up my feelings to Zach during our sessions. I told myself that it had been an isolated incident, but even if the moment had been all in my head, I wasn't as comfortable discussing my sex life with Zach as I'd once been. Knowing that my body had responded to someone besides my husband felt like a betrayal. Not only to Chris but to myself. I was working so hard to get us back to a good place but apparently my body had plans of its own. Was I really that lonely? Or had the thought of sex with Chris become so confusing that I was now hyperaware? It wasn't like being attracted to Zach was without its own set of baggage, but I almost preferred it to my sex life with Chris.

Zach was a handsome man, he always had been. I'd be lying if I said that I'd never seen him in that light but it had always been a secondary observation. Something that had no bearing on my life. When we'd first met he'd been so much older than me that it had never mattered and by the time we met up again Chris and I were married. It was uncomfortable being made aware of him as a man when we'd been acquaintances for so long. It meant that there was an undercurrent whenever I went to his office that had been missing before.

I liked his hands.

The size of them, the graceful dance of his fingers as he gripped his pen or gestured as he talked always caught my eye. During quiet moments I found my imagination wondering, picking up little details that I'd always been aware of but had never acknowledged. It's like knowing that the sky is blue or that water is wet. The mole under his left eye was a way of life, just as much so as his carefully trimmed fingernails and the precise way he did his hair every day. I found myself fascinated by the gray stubble that darkened his jaw whenever he went a few days without shaving and on more than one occasion I wondered what it would feel like against the palm of my hand. Was his hair softer than Chris's or more wiry? My curiosity kept me occupied in moments of otherwise boredom.

A way of life, until abruptly, unwittingly, they were all I could pay attention to.

Has his voice always been that deep? Probably. But hearing him laugh had never given me goosebumps before. My body seemed to have a mind of its own. The more dismal my sex life with Chris became, the more details about Zach I seemed to notice. It got to the point where even standing too close to him could make my body grow warm. I wasn't proud of myself for my reaction but I didn't necessarily hate it either. It had been so long since I'd felt attractive or wanted that I couldn't fault my instincts. It was exciting and – since I had no intention of giving into temptation and exploring those feelings – innocent.

It would have been simpler to say 'no' whenever Chris expressed interest in me physically, but there was always a surge of guilt afterward for turning him down. He was my husband and it was one of the few moments of true intimacy that we shared anymore. I enjoyed the illicit thrill of my silent, seeming one-sided interest with Zach, but that's where things came to a screeching halt for me. Actually having sex, at least sex with Chris, was an exercise in emotional endurance. Most of my time was spent going through the motions. In bed, where it counted, when it mattered the most, I couldn't get excited at all. Rather than anticipation when Chris started to exhibit those all too familiar hints about what was on his mind, I was instead filled with dread. When it was all said and done, Chris rolled away satisfied while I was left feeling like a failure as a woman and as a wife. I told myself that I was supposed to enjoy myself, that there was something wrong with me because I couldn't, that I was overthinking things and getting in my own way, that I…

That I…

What are you supposed to do when everything you try seems to be wrong? How can you possibly hope to make things better when it's nearly impossible to roll out of bed every morning? It was juvenile really, that something so simple could cut so deeply. That something so natural could leave me scrambling and anxious.

Sex was supposed to be the easy part. It *used* to be the easy part. Chris was still doing all the things he used to and I knew that if I could only get my head on straight that I would enjoy myself. But I couldn't, and the more I tried the harder it became to try the next time. Insecurity fed on doubt and doubt watered more of my insecurities. It was a cycle I couldn't break from and the fact that Chris didn't see it, that he didn't seem to notice or care, was just proof that my suspicions weren't as unfounded as I might have hoped.

The thoughts went on endlessly, an ongoing cycle of self-doubt and frustration that soon left me dreading the idea of sex entirely. There was so much pressure on me to perform regardless of how I may feel afterward. It eroded my self-confidence because I couldn't help but wonder if Chris even cared about how I felt or if he was only concerned with making sure that he 'got off.' I even tried bringing it up a time or two but he grew so offended at the accusation that he only came to me for sex that it usually devolved into an argument that left me crying and emotionally drained.

I've always struggled with my sense of worth and this particular issue between Chris and me fed on every insecurity that I had. It got so bad that I often found myself wondering if it even mattered *who* he was sleeping with. After all, it's not like I could call what we were doing 'making love.' Instead it felt as if I were a tool, something Chris used to masturbate. Of no more importance than a bottle of lotion or a box of Kleenex. Which, if true, meant that I was just as easily replaced.

It was painful enough having these kinds of doubts, but having them about – and because of – my own husband was somehow worse. He was supposed to be my safe space, the person I went to to remind myself what it is to know love unconditionally. Because I couldn't talk about how I was feeling with him without being put on the spot, I went along with things in an attempt not to make our relationship any more tense than it needed to be. Once we were in therapy, I'd promised myself that I wouldn't let things go simply because it was easier than confronting them. Even so, I had to accept the fact that I would need to pick my battles. If I brought up everything that bothered me all the time I was afraid that the legs on which our marriage stood would crumble into dust.

Chris and I couldn't afford to flounder, not with kids to think about. So much time had gone into our relationship, so many years of happy memories still lay beneath our belt, that I was sure that it would be enough to fall back on when everything else seemed too overwhelming. The problem is that almost every day seemed too overwhelming and – with little choice in the matter – I found myself mentioning our problems in the bedroom with Zach.

By the time I'd worked up the courage to broach the subject, I'd analyzed our last run-in from every possible angle. Time had softened the intensity of the moment and it was easier to convince myself that I'd read something into it that had never been there in the first place. His expression had brought me up short. There had been sympathy there, a flash of anger on my behalf, and then he was back to exuding neutrality.

"Have you spoken to him about any of this?"

I shrugged and glanced down at my lap. "I try. It's just that…" Blowing out a shaky breath, I hesitated. "I can't always express myself the way that I want when I'm trying to get my point across. I'll plan out what I want to say and how I want to say it, but as soon as I open my mouth things go off the rails."

"Why do you think that is?" he queried.

Sighing, I settled more comfortably in my seat. We'd been talking for several minutes already but there was still an hour to go before my session was up. "I don't know why. Not for sure. It could be Chris, or maybe he's right and I really am too emotional."

Or maybe it was a combination of the two.

"There's nothing wrong with being emotional," Zach mused, breaking my reverie. "Emotional intelligence is just as important as book smarts or street smarts. If you're in tune with how you feel, it's something to be proud of since not everyone is capable of that kind of self-reflection."

My jaw nearly hit the floor. This was the first time anyone had complimented me for something many viewed as a personal flaw. I didn't know what to do with his words and mentally I scrambled for something to say, something to undermine the moment's weight so it didn't seem so important. Was it really a mark of self-reflection? Of personal awareness? I didn't understand how it possibly could be. More often than not it more closely resembled exactly what Chris was always accusing me of.

"You're still not used to compliments, are you?"

I glanced up, realizing belatedly that I'd looked away at the first kind word. "What do you mean?"

Zach tapped his pen on the edge of his notebook. "You don't like it when someone says something nice about you."

"It's not that I don't like it," I admitted carefully. "I'm just not used to it."

It's not the first time someone had told me that but coming from Zach the assessment sat much differently with me. There was an air of truth to it that I couldn't ignore. I'd never been great with compliments. They made me uncomfortable and it was hard to determine why. Saying that I wasn't used to them wasn't necessarily true. I've been complimented before. Chris used to do it all the time.

"You don't think you deserve them?"

That brought me up short. Was that really all there was to it? When I dug below the surface I realized that he had hit the nail on the head. I didn't think I deserved the nice things people said to me. The comments seemed disingenuous because I was so used to talking down to myself. Praise had never seemed all that important before, but I realized that I couldn't expect to go through life berating myself without craving positive affirmations from *someone*.

The rest of the session was spent with Zach talking to me about what I liked about myself and what sort of image I thought I presented to the rest of the world. It was uncomfortable work, and in the end I groaned in a mix of rising frustration and desperation that we couldn't drop the topic entirely.

"What does any of this matter?" I muttered irritably. "I thought we were talking about my sex life."

Zach smiled, and for a moment I was reminded of our time back in high school, when he was one of my few emotional pillars in a time when I needed them the most.

"We are. Just not directly." When I didn't respond he went on. "We create boundaries out of a sense of self-worth. If you don't believe that you deserve better then you won't demand better from those around you. I'll need Chris to come in so that we can discuss his side of things, but a big part of enjoying sex comes from feeling good about yourself and knowing that the person you're with values you. These last few weeks, Chris hasn't done anything either physically or emotionally to show whether he does or not." His lips tightened with annoyance and there was a flash of compassion in his gaze that softened my proverbial hackles. "It's no wonder you haven't been enjoying sex."

I wasn't sure how to respond to that, so I didn't say anything at all. Thankfully, my hour was up and it was time to run some errands before heading back home. I took my time because, if possible, I dreaded walking through my front door even more than usual. Whenever Zach and I discussed something new there was always this moment of anticipation and nervousness at the thought of having to address it with Chris. Zach had told me once more that he would like to bring up the issue during my next joint session with my husband and I'd been dreading it ever since. Somehow, I'd managed to convince myself that if I could linger in the grocery store debating on which box of cereal to buy for long enough that I could put it off indefinitely.

But no such luck.

Eventually I would have to come back to reality; go home and clean, cook dinner tonight, play with my children, and try and reconnect with Chris on some level before going to bed exhausted. Then I would wake up tomorrow and start the whole thing all over again from the beginning. Throughout the day and into the next I fought back the yawning chasm swimming in the center of my chest. Despite Zach's encouragement, or maybe because of it, I was painfully aware of just how alone I was in all of this.

Marriage is a partnership, but where do you turn when the person you're supposed to overcome obstacles with *is* the obstacle? Chris and I shared many of the same friends and I didn't want to put them in the awkward position of knowing more about our personal problems than they were comfortable with. I also didn't like casting Chris in a bad light when he was such a good, if misguided, man. For the most part I tried to keep the details about what went on in our bedroom between myself, Chris, and Zach.

The joint session with Chris went about as well as expected. With a pointed glance from Zach I was able to broach the topic in question yet again. As usual, Chris seemed genuinely confused and hurt.

"That's not true," he denied shortly. "You know I love you. If there was ever a time when I made you feel as if I only wanted you for sex…" He shook his head, throat working as he calmed himself back down. "That was never my intention, Bri."

I relaxed by slow degrees. We had been working with Zach on acknowledging how the *other* person felt without undermining their feelings with qualifiers. It wasn't perfect but the fact that he made the effort left me hopeful that something was getting through. I was wrong, of course. There were moments of clarity when the old Chris showed through and his compassion and care for me outweighed his knee-jerk reaction to deny responsibility. The fact that Zach was there as backup may have had something to do with his acquiescence but all too soon he was contradicting himself.

"—as if she's never in the mood anymore," he griped at one point, glancing at me from the corner of his eye. "Of course I'm upset."

I get it. I really do. Sex is an important part of many relationships. I didn't fault Chris for wanting to be intimate with me, but it often came across as the *only* thing he cared about. Zach assured me that I held more value beyond just the physical and it was frustrating that Chris seemed incapable, or unwilling, to connect with me intimately in any way beyond sex.

While Chris claimed during that session and many of the sessions that followed that my fears were misplaced, his behavior at home remained the same. He said one thing only to contradict himself later with complaints about our sex life. As had become the norm for him, Chris didn't seem inclined to make any real changes to make things better between us.

Chapter Six

There's a peculiar sort of loneliness that comes from untapped vulnerability. It's like seeing a box with the word *'fragile'* written on the side. You know that there's something breakable hidden away and you want to reach out, to touch it, to admire it, but it isn't yours to have. I should have come with a warning label; though I doubt that would have stopped people from handling me so carelessly, There was a well of something brewing within me, a hunger for intimacy that grew as first weeks and then months passed. My attraction to Zach only grew as the situation at home remained stagnant. I craved something and, almost like a dance, my attention circled around the one person who seemed capable of fulfilling that craving.

The little things that I had begun to notice had grown in number. It was no longer just a lone freckle or an errant chuckle that captured my attention. It was the easy, confident way he sat across from me. It was the breadth of his shoulders and the sharp cut of his jaw. It was in the steady way he regarded me, and the compassion and patience in his voice when we spoke. I started to look forward to my sessions with Zach for other reasons than the hope it offered my marriage. He was no longer just a friendly presence or a source of comfort and understanding. He was…a man.

Almost two months after Zach opened up to me about his divorce, a close friend of mine named Deandra told me that she had run into him while she was out to dinner one night. I felt a thrill right until she casually mentioned the fact that he'd been on a date at the time. I fought back the urge to ask her what his 'date' looked like. It was bad enough that the news hurt so badly. I'd suspected that my feelings were getting out of hand but this confirmed it. The fact that he was seeing someone shouldn't have bothered me either way; *I* was the one who was married after all. As a divorcee it would have been stranger if Zach *hadn't* started dating by now.

I tried to remain casual as I probed her for more details but I felt anything but. Dee and I had gone to the same high school so when Zach realized who she was the two of them had fallen into easy conversation. Dee was surprised to hear that Zach was seeing Chris and me about our marriage issues. I was able to play the situation off, but it still bothered me that he would reveal such a personal fact. What happened to doctor/patient confidentiality? I spoke with friends about how the slipup was odd, but was able to justify it quickly enough.

For the next few days, the knowledge that he was seeing someone weighed more heavily on me than the professional breach of trust. There had been no harm done and I'm sure he'd been surprised to see Dee again after so long and the truth had simply come out. That was easier to explain away than the woman he'd been with, however, and I couldn't help but wonder who she was and what she'd looked like. How long had they been dating, or had dinner been their first and last time out together? Agonizing over Zach's sex life forced me to admit the truth to myself as nothing else could have. I kept thinking that if I didn't say something about my feelings now, then I would lose my chance to say anything at all.

I was clearly an idiot. It was the only explanation. Who else develops a crush on their marriage counselor? Like everything else in my life, trying to talk myself out of what I was feeling or denying it didn't make it go away. If anything, trying to deprive it of oxygen and attention only made it grow stronger. Something needed to change. I couldn't concentrate on healing my marriage when I was constantly thinking about Zach. Though I knew that, I couldn't seem to exorcise my feelings for him no matter how inappropriate I knew they were. With no resolution in sight and guilt a tight band around my chest, I turned to Rachel a week after hearing from Dee.

I didn't seek her out for her advice so much as stumble blindly into it. We were hanging out one night drinking when the truth slipped out. I tried to make it into a joke, hoping a dash of self-deprecation would be enough to distract from the very real hitch in my voice.

Going to my best friend about a boy I had feelings for reminded me of when I was back in high school, but there was no help for it. I needed to talk to someone about how I felt, but more than that I needed her to tell me to get over it. Rachel was much more pragmatic than Tiffany, and that's what I needed at the moment: an outside source telling me that there was no hope and to let this go. To lecture me about analyzing every smile, every glance, every word.

Subconsciously, I was probably counting on Rachel to be the voice of reason. I needed a port in the storm, a life jacket, anything to keep me from sinking any faster than I already was. I was surprised when she laughed and shook her head.

"Duh, Bri." When I gaped, she took a swig of her beer and rolled her eyes. "Sorry. Harsh. But come on." Though we were in the garage she lowered her voice regardless, as if Chris somehow had superhuman hearing. "The guy's older, handsome, and he's been hanging on every word you have to say for months now. I'm honestly surprised you didn't realize that you had a thing for him before now."

Burying my face in my hands to disguise my embarrassment, I spoke through my fingers, voice muffled. "What am I supposed to do?"

The question was mostly rhetorical.

Mostly.

I'd take any advice I could get at this point if it meant getting over Zach. My life was already complicated enough and I didn't have the time or the energy to spend on whatever it was that I was feeling for him. Between Chris and my overall sense of discontent, my emotions were already tied in knots. My sessions with Zach were my only oasis from that, the only place I could go where the thought of the future filled me with hope instead of dread. Chris may never change his ways, but when I was in Zach's office, I could convince myself that he might.

One day.

I could lose all of that, for what? A man with a nice ass and big hands?

"Fuck it." Rachel lifted one shoulder in a shrug. "I think you should tell him."

A bolt of adrenaline left my hands shaking and I sucked in a sharp breath before I could stop myself. "That's not funny."

"I wasn't joking." Her brow furrowed as she frowned. "Think about it," Rachel continued. "Most crushes are built on hope, no matter how far-fetched. You're miserable because you're unsure. The sooner you talk to him, the sooner he can shoot you down. Then you can cry for a few days and get over it."

I hated to admit it, but she was right. Zach brushed my fingers with his own the other day when I handed him my payment after our session and I spent the rest of the day thinking about it; a part of me wondered if he had done it on purpose, while the rest of me hoped that he had.

A definite 'no' would be a much-needed dose of reality.

Even so, something about the idea bothered me. I would miss feeling this way about someone. The first blush of romance is always the best: when a couple is so in love that they can see bits and pieces of one another in the world around them. The constant rush, like electricity swimming in your veins. I didn't want to have feelings for Zach, but being with him reminded me of how things used to be between Chris and me, when the world was still full of promise and anything was possible. It was as if being next to the right person made you stronger somehow, and I needed that sense of strength more than ever with my relationship in turmoil. It was strange. I was lusting after another man to boost my morale so that I could keep fighting to save my marriage.

The problem was that I knew, deep down, that there was much more to it than that. At first I'd reasoned that since nothing would ever come of my feelings then there was no harm being done. Then I found myself comparing Chris to Zach, and I knew that I was trying to justify crossing a line. No one likes to admit that they may have done something reprehensible, and I was no different. I wanted to make excuses, to forgive myself for what I'd thought for so long was a victimless crime. Just because Chris didn't know didn't mean that I wasn't betraying him in a fundamental way. Yes, Zach made me feel special and important. Yes, just being near him was enough to awaken things within me that not even a session with Chris could compete with. Zach was both romantic nostalgia in the way he reminded me of that first flush of true love, and titillating present.

A guilty pleasure like chocolate ice cream or satin panties.

What hurt the most was his kindness. I didn't want to give up on the comradery between us, but I knew that unless I did something to get rid of my feelings for him, I wouldn't have a choice. I was already looking at female psychologists just in case, though I hated the thought of having to start all over again with someone new.

As embarrassing as it may be, Rachel's idea held merit.

'I can do this.' My stomach was twisting into knots, a snake recoiling, as I sat down one day and composed a letter. Writing down all my feelings as they came to me was almost therapeutic. I was finally able to put into words all the things that had been brewing within me over the last several weeks. In a way, it was freeing. I should have stopped there, but I was still riding high off the knowledge that he might be out there, with another woman. Rachel's advice gave me courage, helped me feel as if I wasn't making a total mistake. Once the letter was done to my satisfaction, I transferred my words from paper to text. I wanted to make sure that everything was just right. If I was going to take this step, it may as well convey everything I wanted it to. Then, I pulled up Zach's contact information.

'It's like ripping off a Band-Aid, remember?'

We were both adults. Zach had always been so understanding, and surely this would be no different. Even though I expected nothing more than a polite rejection, once the floodgates opened there was no turning back. I *had* to send it now. After all, I'd just poured out my heart; there was no going back from that. If nothing else, simply getting all of it out there felt better than I would have thought possible. No matter what happened, I'd done what was best for me. Without giving myself time to reconsider, I pressed 'send.'

The wait that followed was agonizing.

On one hand, why hadn't the ground opened up to swallow me whole already? On the other, *why* the hell was it taking him so long to respond? Maybe I'd been too hopeful. What if he hated me now? What if he told me that he couldn't work with Chris and me anymore, given the nature of my feelings? What if he told Chris?

My stomach dropped and I pressed my hand against my middle.

What if?

What if?

What if?

It was my parents' Thanksgiving celebration and I was sitting on a barstool in their basement as the possibilities ran through my head. It was a chilling mantra stuck forever on repeat, and by the time my phone dinged to herald a new message, I was wound so tightly that I practically jumped out of my skin. This was it, the moment of truth. The response I'd waited hours for. I held my breath as I pulled up the message only to stare at my screen in dumbfounded disbelief.

A smirk emoji.

After all of that, all the agonizing and soul searching, that was the first thing that hit me. I'd written him a novel worthy of Harlequin and all he gives me in return is a smirk and the words *'Let's talk tomorrow.'*

I waited, gripping my phone and trying to quell the insidious belief that there would be another text to follow. Something to clarify the ominous obscurity of his response, but there was nothing. Even so, I couldn't quell my excitement. It may not have been a 'yes,' but the most important part was that for all its brevity, it wasn't a 'no' either. Rachel broke away from the festivities long enough to wander over to my side. I showed her the text, brimming with excitement and rising hope and to my delight, her eyes widened and she nearly choked on her beer.

"Are you serious?" she whispered, and I nodded, glancing around and pulling her deeper into the basement to make sure we weren't overheard.

"What do you think he's going to say?"

I had no idea of course, but that didn't stop the two of us from speculating for the rest of the evening. Sleep that night came in fits and spurts. I was so busy agonizing over every little thing that I'd said, going back over my message and trying to see my words from his perspective. I was convinced that if I could just put myself in his shoes then I could uncover some hidden meaning in the text. Playing translator was such exhausting work that even though I wasn't tired, my body snatched what little rest it could before morning. There are only so many emotional hoops a person can jump through before feelings have to take a backseat to more practical concerns.

Sleep was one of them.

My kids were the other.

The next morning dawned like any other except I had this weight that was part dread and part anticipation wrapping a band around my chest as I went about my routine. I barely noticed Chris leaving for work and the boys and their chatter was white noise compared to the doubts swimming through my mind. When my phone rang, I practically leapt to answer it. The caller ID revealed the caller was exactly who I'd hoped and feared it would be. While the kids ate pancakes, I snuck into my bathroom and answered with a tentative "Hello?"

Has my voice always been that small? That unsure? I sounded painfully young, even to myself and I cringed at the thought that Zach would see me and my confession as nothing more than a sign of immaturity, or worse, a sign that I was crazy or desperate. I could deal with a lot of things, but I'd hate it if he didn't take me seriously. For most of my life people had dismissed me and my words, leaving me feeling as if what I had to say and think was of no value. It was a major point of contention in my marriage and I wasn't sure how I'd react if Zach took up that mantle. He was one of the few people who'd never made me feel small or stupid, and I hated the thought that this one thing would be what tipped the scales of his opinion about me. I'd rather be shot down as a woman who knew her heart than brushed aside like a child with a crush. My stomach twisted in knots and my mouth went dry. Sending that text the night before was looking like more and more of a mistake.

"Bri…" Just that, the sound of my name coming out of his mouth, was enough to send a rush through me. A surge of warmth that stretched from the top of my head to the soles of my feet, lingering deliciously in my middle. My face warmed and on the heels of excitement returned the dread it had so valiantly fought back just seconds before. It would be a relief to finally hear him reject me at this point; I didn't think my nerves could take much more of waiting. I couldn't remember ever feeling this nervous about anything before. Not just because Zach was about to shoot me down, but because of what this would mean for Chris and me moving forward. After agonizing over various outcomes for most of the night, I'd come to the conclusion that there was no way that we'd be able to continue working with Zach. For the first time in years there was a glimmer of hope for Chris and me and I'd let my heart get in the way.

I should have known better, but there was no denying my excitement and pleasure at hearing Zach's voice and knowing that, in that small moment, he was all mine and no one else's. He wasn't my therapist; he wasn't an old friend or an adult to rely upon. He was just Zach, and I was just Bri. Breaking down the walls that had stood between us for so long should have been frightening; and it was. But mostly it was just satisfying in a way that I couldn't fully appreciate with my nerves riding me.

'Yeah, it's nice now. Just wait until he tells you he doesn't want you. If you ever step foot in his office again, things are going to be so—'

I shoved the thought aside. It and ones like it had been plaguing me since before I left my parents. If Zach decided to wash his hands of me as a client, I would understand. At this point, the best I could hope for was that Zach wouldn't allow my faux pas to undermine our friendship. It would likely be awkward for a while, but in all fairness, it would have been just as awkward had I spent the foreseeable future pining silently after a man I could never have. At least this way I could go back to focusing on what was truly important.

"Bri…" Though it felt as if hours had passed since he spoke my name, only a few seconds had ticked by. My mind was racing a mile a minute, thoughts flitting to the forefront only to be shoved aside by the next, and then the next. It was exhausting and distracting. Worst of all, it only made me even more jittery. I took a seat on the edge of the tub, curling in over my phone slightly as if I could muffle the sound of his voice from any curious children with body and willpower alone. Which was insane. The kids couldn't hear me, let alone Zach. Even if they could, they wouldn't understand what was going on. Still, guilt and fear had activated a type of fight-or-flight response within me. There would be no fighting, and lowering my voice like a child with a secret was as close to running as I would get in the suburbs without unpacking yoga pants and a sports bra from the depths of my dresser.

Without realizing it, my leg began to bounce. "You don't have to say anything," I found myself interrupting him in a rush. Wincing, I shook my head at myself. After waiting all this time for an explanation, why stop him before he could get a word in edgewise? Maybe because there was no good outcome to all of this. Maybe because hearing him turn me down *was* a best-case scenario since the alternative…

Oh, God, the alternative…

My heart pounded painfully in my chest. "I'm sorry," I continued in a rush. My mind was all over the place. I couldn't think about what would happen if Zach didn't tell me 'no.' I couldn't even fathom what that road would look like. No, I wanted and needed him to be the voice of reason, even if that meant breaking my heart in the process. I was a big girl after all; heartbreak was something I was used to. "I know I put you in a shitty position by saying what I did." I tried to add some amusement to my tone, but I knew he could probably see right through the thin veneer of normalcy as easily as I could hear it within myself. "Believe me," I continued, "I certainly don't expect you to—"

"Brianna." There was something about his tone in that moment. In the way he shaped the letters of my name as if he couldn't help but smile as he did so. I thought of the emoji he'd sent and imagined him smirking as he waited for me to get control of all the nervous energy that had sent my words crashing into one another like ocean waves. "You're fine. Everything is fine. I called because I wanted you to explain what I read. Context can be tricky through text."

'Says the man who responded to a declaration of love with a smirk emoji.'

Swallowing hard, I got to my feet and paced the few steps to the door and back to the tub. I wasn't sure how much more obvious I could have been. I'd spent hours composing that letter making sure every word was just right. A part of me suspected that his request had more to do with confirmation than it did clarification. Still, just in case there was any question about where I stood, I decided to give it a try.

For several seconds I struggled with what to say, but in the end simplicity came to my rescue. "I have feelings for you." It was strange how something so innocuous could set off a maelstrom of anxiety. My tendency to avoid confrontation meant that I often found that it was easier to express my feelings through writing than it was talking about them aloud. When it came to face-to-face interactions, there was so much pressure to say the first thing that came to mind. There was never any time to think something through, to turn it over and examine it for holes or minefields that could trip me up or blow things out of proportion. I knew firsthand how much damage a careless word or awkward phrasing could cause, and jotting down my thoughts and impressions first helped me unpack more complex feelings.

The more I understood 'why' and 'how' I was feeling a certain way, the better I was at conveying my viewpoint to other people. It was hard to tell if this was something that had always been a part of my personality, or if I'd cultivated it over the years as a defense mechanism against constantly being silenced. It was something I'd been working on both at home and during my sessions with Zach and Chris. If I couldn't say what I was feeling aloud, in the moment – when it counted the most – then how was I supposed to change the toxic dynamic that had developed between Chris and me?

I was surprised to find that saying the words aloud, to him, was almost liberating. There was no hiding behind the relative anonymity of the screen and there would be no breathless wait for his response. The cat was well and truly out of the bag. Again. "I wanted to say something because…" Here, I took a deep breath to gather the remainder of my courage. This was the part where he accused me of being delusional. "I sensed that you might feel something for me too."

"That's what I thought," he responded, and this time there was no hint of a smile in his words. Zach sighed and my heart lodged in my throat. "You know, Bri," he continued. "I have to be careful here, but I'd be lying if I said you were wrong."

I nearly dropped my damn phone.

"Wh-what does that mean?" I was stuttering and I didn't even care. My words were clumsy with disbelief. "Do I have to stop seeing you? Does this mean we could talk or hang out with one another outside of your office?" And the questions I didn't voice aloud, *'Was my marriage over?'* and, perhaps just as devastating: *'Was this considered an affair?'*

"Calm down," he said soothingly. "I don't have all the answers yet. All I do know is that I need to see you."

My skin was buzzing, I felt like a live wire, as if the slightest touch would set me and the world alike ablaze. I made a sound low in the back of my throat, something squeaky that was part shock and disbelief and all reckless excitement, and pulled my cell away from my mouth long enough to get myself back under control. Even though I knew this was the worst possible outcome, the satisfaction rushing through me told a different story, blinding me to the reality of the line the two of us had just crossed.

I'm not sure how long we talked after that. Not very because I eventually left the bathroom to go check on the kids. Definitely long enough for me to learn that Zach had been struggling with his own feelings for months now. If I hadn't said anything, he may have never guessed that we were going through the same things. I tried to ignore the implication of that, to divest myself of the weighty responsibility of knowing I'd set a ball in motion that should have remained still. Guilt could, and would, come later. For now I wanted to ride the high of this new intimacy, of the way his voice deepened an octave as we spoke, of the way butterflies danced in my stomach when we promised to revisit the topic in person when we met for our next session in a few days.

When we hung up, I stood clutching my phone, still in disbelief that any of that had just happened. But no. It was right there, fresh in my memory. Every soft word, every errant chuckle, everything. I would go on to replay our conversation over and over again that day, distracted from my usual routine by the anticipation and wonder of it all. Nothing bothered me as much that day and the world seemed brighter, somehow. Not so much because of Zach, I realized. But because of what he represented.

Change.

Excitement.

Something *more* than what I'd grown used to after years of doing and saying the same things day in and day out. There was fear too, definitely that, but in the shadow of this new truth, even that held an edge of promise. There would be consequences for this. There always was when it came to doing something forbidden, but I wasn't scared. Not yet. Like a wild thing I could taste freedom on the edge of my tongue and there was no stopping me from rushing headlong in pursuit.

Chapter Seven

My hands were shaking and my chest was uncomfortably tight. I sat in the parking lot outside of Zach's office for God knows how long before I finally dredged up the courage to go into the building and up the now familiar set of stairs. A week had passed since we spoke over the phone and I was anxious to see him face-to-face. Time had dulled some of my certainty and I was back to being just as nervous and unsure as I'd been before he admitted to his own feelings. Could he have been humoring me? Zach wasn't a liar, but maybe he'd been tempted to tell me what I wanted to hear in the moment. Maybe he felt sorry for me? None of what I feared made any sense, but that didn't stop me from thinking that way regardless.

I hesitated a moment before knocking on his office door, jumping when it opened only a second later. It was as if he'd been waiting on me. Perhaps he had been. I wavered between flattery and feeling flustered. I'd been hoping to have a few seconds to catch my breath, but no such luck. All too soon, he was standing before me and he seemed larger than life, more imposing than I ever remember him being. I was aware of him in a way that my body was still trying to get used to, in a way that it liked. This new version of Zach was distracting in a way that I'd never truly appreciated before and my skin, already warm with embarrassment and nerves, flushed a deeper red. His lips twitched and he motioned me inside, studying my face before allowing his eyes to linger on the rest of my body. Ducking my head, I darted past him, careful not to let our bodies touch in the narrow space of the doorway. This was our opportunity to talk things through and I knew if I touched him, even in passing, that I'd be too distracted to think of doing much else.

"Bri, how are you today?"

Pleasantries.

Great.

My mouth was as dry as the Sahara and he wanted to exchange pleasantries as if this was just any other day. I would have laughed if I knew it wouldn't come out an anxious croak. I kept telling myself that there was no reason why I should be so scared. The worst was technically over. I'd put myself out there in a very big way and it had actually gone well. Several days had passed and Zach had yet to retract his words. In fact, he was standing before me, relaxed and smiling. No hint of regret or ulterior motive. This was the first time I'd ever put my feelings on the line like this before. I wasn't an assertive person by any means and the risk of rejection was still a weight hanging over my head, ready to crash down at any moment. I was waiting for that other shoe to drop, to prove my darkest fears correct.

Never in my wildest dreams would I have imagined myself standing here, anxiously waiting for Zach to address the elephant in the room. He made me brave. Or stupid. Either way, ever since the two of us had reconnected I'd begun to step further and further outside of my comfort zone. Doing things I wouldn't have credited myself with the courage to pull off. Confronting Chris had been the start of it all, and though things were more tense in my life I *liked* this new, bolder version of myself. It made me feel stronger, as if I could take on anything.

Have anything.

Or rather, anyone.

That's why I was here, wasn't it?

Not just to discuss our 'situation' but because I wanted to entertain the thought that I could have Zach in some sort of tangible way. That I could cement this thing between us in stone, make it real.

'What about Chris?'

Strange. All week, and even during the ride to Zach's office, Chris had been at the forefront of my mind. Now? Now he seemed all too distant, a side player in something much larger and more complex. I tried to remind myself of what it was I was supposed to be fighting for, but it was too late.

It was just him and me. As was the case every time I came to his office to talk, nothing else outside these walls existed. Despite my anxiety that something could go wrong at any minute, I relaxed by slow degrees. I could trust Zach. I was never too shy or too scared to tell him anything, and this was no different. He was my rock, the one person I could truly count on to be there for emotional support. Here, with him, I was allowed to be vulnerable. To be scared and unsure without losing a part of myself. It allowed me the long-coveted freedom of fully expressing myself without caring about the censure that might follow. It was a fantasy world when I was in that room, and without realizing it, my body gave in to the magic of it. I took my first deep breath since that morning and managed to quell my jitters enough to take a seat across from him.

I'd dressed very carefully that morning in a maroon backless sweater with skinny jeans and black combat boots. The edge of sex appeal had given me the courage to come to his office and the way he looked at me with heavy-lidded eyes – dark with appreciation – made me glad I'd chosen to show a little skin despite the chill in the air.

"So," I began, unable to stand his quiet scrutiny any longer. Crossing one leg over the other I strove to keep my voice light. "What now?"

"What do you mean?" he queried, blue eyes unwavering.

I shrugged. "I mean, where do we go from here?" Shaking my head, I lifted a hand to fidget with the ends of my hair only to let it fall once more. "I know you wanted to talk, but I'm not sure what more needs to be said."

One brow lifted in what I could have sworn was a challenge and my heart skipped a beat.

"Who said anything about talking?"

Lips parting I could feel my cheeks warm. Damn it. Right when I'd finally managed to calm down. "You did." I frowned, thinking back. "Didn't you?"

Zach shook his head and leaned back in his seat, a small smile playing around his lips. "No, actually. I didn't. I said that I wanted to see you this week. Never mentioned a thing about talking."

His gaze cut straight through me, roving over my body as if he could peel back the layer of clothes separating my skin from those blue depths. Hunger and longing stirred deep within me, battling for dominance, and my breath caught. If I hadn't already fallen for him, I would have done so again at that moment. Zach was the only person who could look at me and make me feel as if he truly saw me for who I was instead of who he thought I should be. There was no hiding or pretense with him; there never had been. He'd always been the one person in the world unafraid to reflect my soul right back to me, to show me the cracks and hand me the tools to fix them. It struck me that this man and I had been connected for years, not just as acquaintances and friends but as kindred spirits. I didn't know much about his personal life, but the little I did know painted an all too familiar picture. Zach had been adopted and I recognized a lost soul when I saw one, a person who had spent their lives trying to figure out where they belonged. Someone who never felt good enough. Someone who was always striving to emotionally connect with another person and failing when it mattered most.

I knew Zach without ever needing to hear his entire story because I recognized parts of myself within him. They drew us together like magnets, an inescapable force of nature. My hands were shaking and I swallowed hard, trying one more time to bring us both back on track.

"About Chris—"

"Bri," he interrupted. "Not now." I clamped my mouth shut and watched as he lifted a hand, beckoning me towards him. "Come here."

There's nothing I wanted more than to stand and cross those few feet between us, but I remained in my seat. Apprehension was a heavy weight and I shifted in my seat, fingers twisting among themselves. Anxiety warned that this was all just a test. Was I really allowed to cross those boundaries? What was going to happen when I did? Did I want to find out badly enough to put everything, including my marriage, on the line?

This wasn't how I'd imagined this meeting going. We were supposed to sit and learn more about one another, perhaps delve into exactly why I was so drawn to him and vice versa. He would tell me more about his wife, his family, and I would be the one listening for once. The one watching someone else crack themselves open. It was only fair. He knew everything about me; never had I held anything back about myself or my thoughts. I wanted that from Zach. Craved it with an intensity that surprised me. Not that it should have. Wasn't it only natural to want to learn as much about a person you've grown to care for? This was doubly true for me because I'd known Zach for so long and yet, he'd always remained an enigma.

Maybe it was presumptuous to think that he would start spilling intimate details about himself during our first ever tête-à-tête, but I'd at least hoped to learn what his favorite color was and what sort of foods he liked. If nothing else, I wouldn't have been shocked if I'd shown up only for him to tell me that I needed to find a new therapist. I was prepared for either of those eventualities. Those were scenarios I'd run through in my mind over and over again. I thought I'd come prepared, that I was ready. But I hadn't anticipated what those eyes would do to me. How they would lure me in close as if he were a snake charmer showing off his prowess.

Without thought, I went to him, gasping as he pulled me close. He exuded warmth and I found myself sinking into his lap instinctively. The scent of him, all skin and warmth and cologne, surrounded me and suddenly, nothing else mattered but this.

This.

His lips against mine, strong and sure. Both demanding and achingly gentle. I met his tongue with my own, shuddering as his fingers delved into my hair. He cradled my head, held me in place so that he could explore my mouth one delicious inch at a time. His brown leather chair squeaked beneath our combined weight and my eyes drifted shut. For all his experience, it wasn't a great kiss. Mainly because I was in shock that it was happening at all. I was making out with my therapist. With *Zach*. For years Chris had been the only man to touch me and there was a moment of awkwardness on my part as I tried to shake old habits and reacclimate. My body knew how Chris liked to be kissed, how he liked to be touched – but this wasn't Chris and I found myself stumbling, clumsy with lack of familiarity. As had been the case for years now, it was hard to get out of my head long enough to simply exist in the moment. Just as jarring was the fact that it was difficult to reconcile Zach, a man I'd always considered to be older and more mature, an authority figure, with the person currently sticking their tongue down my throat.

He'd been an adult in my eyes for so long that it was nearly impossible to ignore the power he'd always had over me, first in high school and then again as my therapist. I could have cried. The thing I'd been dreaming about for weeks was finally happening and I couldn't even focus on it long enough to enjoy myself.

"Bri." I flinched, surprised to hear the sound of his voice when touch had so easily become the only way to communicate. "Relax." I took a breath, exhaled, allowed the tightness to drain from my shoulders and spine until I was curved into him, lips blossoming beneath the steady pressure of his, a flower or flame, something fierce and beautiful that had previously been primal and hidden.

My eyes fell shut and with his hands a brand against my bare skin, I let my worries fall quiet and my thoughts go still. It was an experiment at first. A moment of silence to test myself, to see if I could keep the anxiety and doubt away. His tongue caressed mine and one second turned into two, then a third and fourth, until time fell away. My nerves were buzzing, my heart pounding in my ears until I was dizzy with pleasure. I haven't felt this way for so long that it was like my body was coming alive for the first time. It was a heat that hit deep and hard, a tug in my womb that stole my breath and left me panting.

This was it, that feeling I'd been searching for in my marriage for years. It was a pleasure so clear and sharp that it left me feeling alive. My teeth nipped Zach's bottom lip, a warning and encouragement all rolled into one and he made a low sound in the back of his throat that tightened things between my legs. Shifting in his lap, I couldn't help but notice the heavy, hard weight of his excitement stretching the front of his pants. Reaching down, I undid his zipper, eager to release him and press skin on skin. To determine if he really was as hard and hot as I thought he was. Zach shuddered when I made contact with his body, fingers roving and curious and I felt a thrill of power. Here, with him, I was wanted, sexy, unstoppable. I wanted more of that feeling more than anything else in the world at that moment and everything became a blur.

One moment fed into the next, a sea of greedy hands and kisses. Zach left a trail of fire down the side of my throat as he teased my nipples and I squirmed, crying out for him even as he lifted me and walked a few feet towards the couch to lay me on my back.

That couch.

How many times had I sat here, clutching one of the small pillows as I spilled my heart out? How many times had I opened myself up, revealing my inner secrets and fears, hoping for just a modicum of understanding? This couch had seen every vulnerable moment, had borne witness to each time Zach had lifted another layer within me to see what I kept hidden beneath. I'd been stripped down and laid bare in every way but this one and now…now the couch would be there for that too.

This was the same couch – my mind noted almost casually – that I'd been sitting on week after week with Chris as we struggled to work through the issues in our marriage. The couch where I thought we might be able to fix what lay so broken between us, but somehow never did. The thought was a fleeting one. I refused to allow it to linger, to set its claws in my mind and cool the inferno blazing between us. This was heaven, a delicious, forbidden sort of pleasure that I was unwilling to ignore. I'd been without for so long that I wasn't sure I could stop even if I'd wanted to. Sex requires a certain amount of give-and-take. The frustrating part was that Chris understood that all too well. When it came to sex – while he was a good lover and knew how to please me – it often felt as if the act itself was the only thing he wanted or needed me for. A lot of what he did for me seemed as if it were more for his own ego rather than any satisfaction he hoped I might feel. I didn't like feeling as if I were only there for sex and, as I've mentioned before, the suspicion that I was nothing more than a tool was a turnoff.

The bedroom was my stage and as long as I played my part and kept what I truly wanted out of the equation, the audience was happy. At some point, sex became a chore to get through. Something I had to mentally prep myself for hours in advance. By now, I was a pro at faking. I knew what Chris wanted from me and I knew how to twine my body around his in order to give it to him. I knew what sounds to make and when to shudder. I knew when and how he would orgasm. My sex life was a carefully constructed blueprint that I had been adding to since long before either of us said 'I do.' It took no heart or great skill on my part, simply a smile and some patience.

This was probably one of the many reasons why Chris was so convinced that nothing was wrong between us. Not because I was so good at faking it, but because he never bothered to investigate beneath the surface. The fault lay with us both and by the time we started seeing Zach and I grew tired of pretending, our communication was too poor to fix what had been broken for so long. It would take time – which I was growing tired of giving – and effort, which Chris refused to expend.

There was no playacting when it came to Zach.

He knew me in ways that my husband didn't. Not because of our history together but because he didn't presume to know what I was thinking or feeling. If he felt hesitancy in the tightness of my muscles or doubt in my kiss, he was there whispering reassurances in my ear. Soothing me with fingers and tongue until I grew pliant beneath him. There was no rush. It seemed as if we had all the time in the world to explore one another, or maybe the novelty of stripping away his clothes and then mine made the world slow down.

Despite the pleasure he offered, there was still a tight ball of tension deep within me. Not because of what I was doing, but because of who I was doing it with. The sight of his jaw, the look in his eyes, the unfamiliar width of his hands, all of it was both unfamiliar and yet striking in its normalcy. Even the scent of him, so long engraved in my mind next to the image of him sitting calmly across from me as he questioned some latent fear or insecurity, boggled the senses.

It's hard to explain the juxtaposition of the moment. My brain had been taught to associate everything I knew about Zach with comfort. He'd been relegated to a certain slot in my mind where I'd thought there would never be any escape. Now, every touch and kiss scrubbed away at years of familiarity and began to paint new pictures.

Walls fell and were rebuilt until only I was left standing, unsure and uncaring which way was up and which was down.

While I couldn't fully relax, that didn't stop me from enjoying what he was doing to me. Pleasure wasn't a suggestion that I could turn away from but rather a full-body experience that became all consuming, each moment building on the next until every inch of me was throbbing like a fresh wound.

"Just relax for me, Bri." His voice against the shell of my ear made me shudder. "Take a deep breath. Let me feel you."

And I did.

He spread my legs, pulling me close so that my calves rested on his shoulders. There was a moment of wild disbelief. There I was, naked in the middle of the day, and about to have sex in my therapist's office. These were the kinds of things you read about in *Penthouse* right next to financially accommodating pizza delivery guys and frisky pool boys. Did that make me a horny, bored housewife? In theory maybe, though I'd never thought of myself that way. There was a moment, before he slipped inside of me, where everything went still and quiet. The world seemed to be holding its breath and so I did too.

Zach thrust within me slowly at first, picking up speed as my body responded in first shudders, and then wracking waves. I lifted my hips for him, meeting his thrusts with my own, gasping as he touched the very center of me with every surge and dip. It was magical. So magical in fact that it cast a spell over everything that had held me back in that parking lot less than an hour before. Poof. Just like that, and it was all gone. Thoughts of Chris, worries about my marriage, fear over what crossing this line could mean.

It seemed alright, almost natural, to be entangled with Zach like this. Sweat melding our skin together even as our breaths merged. Locking eyes with him as he thrust between my legs was just another, deeper kind of penetration. Sex was one thing, but intimacy…So many years had passed since I'd felt truly connected with Chris that I wondered if I even knew how, or what it meant anymore. I thought I'd forgotten what it was like, to bare more than my naked flesh to the man that I was with. Hell, I'd forgotten what it was like to be with someone who wanted to see beneath the surface. Who wanted to witness the gentle destruction that came over me as completion threatened. Who marveled at the way my back arched and my lips parted on a strangled cry as my orgasm ripped through me and left my mind blissfully empty.

There was so much more to sex than getting off, and I'd lost that in between the arguments and the insecurities, the depression and the loneliness. Zach had been delving past my defenses for so long that as I came back down to earth, I could almost believe that all these long months talking to him about my problems had been little else but foreplay. He came, the echo of his satisfied groan lingering against my skin like a kiss and we both collapsed onto the floor in exhaustion, too shaky to try and figure out how to maneuver onto the couch together.

It took a while for my legs to stop shaking. I couldn't recall the last time I'd had an orgasm that I hadn't given myself, and the difference was enough to make me wonder how I'd ever done without. I wanted to curl up and take a nap, but with the completion of the act came the cold light of reality and common sense. A glance at the clock showed me that while my time wasn't yet up, it was getting close to the moment where I would need to leave or risk running into his next client.

That was all the encouragement I needed to clamber for my clothes, though my fingers were clumsy as I dressed and fixed my hair. Beside me Zach pulled on his own clothes, straightening his shirt and slacks until it was impossible to tell that we'd just done anything at all. I reached for my purse but Zach reached for my hand, pulling me up short.

"I should go."

Zach sat on the floor, propping his back up against the couch and leaning his head back on the cushions. Lazily, he smiled and tugged me down next to him.

"Not yet."

"B—"

"Bri." He chuckled, pulling me in close to his side and pressing a gentle kiss to my lips. "It's called the afterglow for a reason. You're supposed to enjoy it."

I was nervous at first, expecting that someone would come through the door and see us together at any moment. Neither one of us had bothered to lock the door, likely because there had been little reason to when we were supposed to be talking. The fact that no one had walked in and caught us was a miracle in itself. If anything, sitting next to him after what we'd just done should have been less nerve-racking, but somehow it wasn't. I was sure that anyone who saw me would be able to tell what we'd been up to. The desire to hide away was strong, but as soon as I was settled beside Zach, my tension disappeared.

I relaxed against him, leaning my head on his shoulder and breathing in his warmth. Enjoying the shiver that went through me at being so close. I enjoyed the way I reacted to his proximity, even after we'd just gotten done having sex. It was amazing how sensitive I was to even the smallest thing now that I was with someone who made me feel wanted. It reminded me of how Chris and I had been when we'd first started dating. Was it just because I was with someone new or was it the man himself? Was it my fault or had Chris and I simply…grown apart? First in the bedroom and then everywhere else.

Now that Chris was back on my mind, it was hard to push him away again.

Taking a deep breath, I swallowed down the budding panic. It would come later – there would be no avoiding it and I could sense it rising within me like something I would drown in – but for now I wanted to enjoy the last few moments we had left. With Zach I was on top of the world, glowing from the inside out.

"I guess this changes everything, huh?" The words were a weight I couldn't escape, but they needed to be said. I wanted to be able to laugh it all off, to pretend as if it wasn't a big deal, but my throat threatened to tighten with tears. It was childish, but I said what I did because I wanted him to deny it. To tell me that everything would go back to normal. That we could pretend that none of this had ever happened.

But Zach had never been the type to sugarcoat the truth.

"I won't be able to treat you anymore," he began. My stomach clenched. "Don't worry." Zach nuzzled the side of my neck. "I'll still be here for you. I wouldn't leave you alone now. But I can't, in good conscience, call myself your therapist after…this."

I gripped his hand, squeezing it while I processed his words. If Zach were no longer in my life, I wasn't sure what I would do. I depended on his steady presence and sage advice. It was the only thing I could count on now that things at home had been thrown upside down.

"Will I still see you?" It was unclear how exactly this new dynamic between us was supposed to work. How could he truly be there for me if he were no longer my therapist? Zach must have sensed my confusion because he answered carefully.

"We'll meet like usual," he began. "I'll still give you advice, just not in an official capacity."

It made sense really. Zach wasn't exactly the best person in the world to counsel me about the issues in my marriage. Not anymore. I never thought of myself as a hypocrite, but I couldn't shake the suspicion that I was toeing that line. How could I work on my marriage at all now, regardless of whether it was with Zach or anyone else? A crush was one thing, that was harmless. But there was no coming back from this. One decision had effectively changed the course of everything. I couldn't fathom just how much or how deeply that change would be felt. It was difficult to even pinpoint exactly what I was feeling at that moment.

Did I want to save my relationship with Chris still? Was there anything even left to save? The uncertainty left a sour taste in my mouth and I shifted uncomfortably. I didn't want to think about Chris, not right now. I'd been doing so well up until this point and I just wanted to enjoy the moment for a little while longer. Before reality could get the chance to push its way back in.

Zach and I spent the next few minutes talking softly and planning for when we'd see one another again. I allowed myself to linger for as long as I could but I knew that it was time for me to leave. As if on cue, my phone rang, and I flinched as I glanced down at it.

"I really have to go." Instead of waiting for a reply, I surged to my feet.

"Everything alright?"

"Uh, yeah." My phone was still ringing but I couldn't look at the caller ID again. Not while Zach was looking directly at me. "Everything's fine. I just need to go and pick up the kids."

It was a lie and we both knew it, but Zach didn't question it. I gathered my purse and hurried towards the door. I couldn't look back at him, I couldn't kiss him goodbye. That ringing was a wordless condemnation and long after my cell fell silent I could hear it echoing in my mind. Zach's arm on my shoulder stopped me before I could step out into the hall. Without a word, he pulled me into his arms, wrapping me in a tight hug that quieted the sudden bout of nerves.

"Next time." His voice was a husky promise and I nodded. I didn't trust my voice to speak so instead I arched into him and let the call go to voicemail. The sex had been good but this…this was irreplaceable. This was gold. Loneliness had been such a loyal companion for so long that I'd grown used to the gaping hope within me, even when I was surrounded by people. Zach's touch filled that emptiness, warmed the cold corners. It was like an all too welcome silence in a sea of noise, an oasis, and I had to fight the urge to stay right where I was. For a few more blissful seconds I was the happiest I could remember being. This tall, solid man made me feel protected in his arms.

It was where I wanted to be.

Where I *needed* to be.

Chapter Eight

I knew better than to believe such a fantasy for long. Zach and I separated and I hurried down the stairs to the parking lot. With every step my legs grew heavier and heavier. The weight that I had worked so hard to shed was returning. It slowed me down, making every step a chore. I wanted to run back to Zach's office, throw myself in his arms, and forget the rest of the world again.

Maybe if I weren't a wife, weren't a mother, I might have done just that. Then again, if I were neither of those things, I never would have had any reason to reconnect with Zach again in the first place.

'Hours,' I thought, breathlessly sliding into my driver's seat. *'I've been gone for hours.'*

My hands shook as I pulled out my phone, staring at my missed call and the name on the display. *Chris.* It was probably nothing but I couldn't stop thinking about what I'd just done and the paranoid part of my brain told me that Chris knew, somehow. I'd always thought of betrayal as something black and white. It was supposed to be cut and dry. The movies I saw and the books I read always painted infidelity as something mired in lust and lies. Something that dealt in selfishness and a lack of empathy or love.

I'd never thought I'd ever have to find out differently, and yet here I was. Sitting in my car, unable to move forward or look back, and trying to figure out what I should say to my husband. Assuming I should say anything at all. He had no idea of what I'd been up to; if I began acting suspiciously wouldn't that change? I'd never done something like this before. I didn't know what to do or say, and I damn sure had no idea how I should feel. Guilt and lingering happiness created a miasma of emotion, too complex to pinpoint or ignore. I loved my husband and my kids, and I never wanted to hurt them. Yet, I'd done the unthinkable. This…this would hurt everyone and everything. If Chris found out it would undo what little progress we'd made at home. Though if I were being honest, would it really cause that much damage? After all, things hadn't improved at home at all. Chris and I were still struggling and the tension between us was just as bad, if not worse, than ever before.

Driving back home, I knew that I was pulling at straws. As much as I might like to think that sleeping with Zach wouldn't make things any worse for Chris and me, the fact was that I knew better. I wanted to find any excuse that I could to ease the weight of what had just happened but there was no escaping the ramifications. Now that I had been with Zach, I couldn't simply forget what it had been like. Nor did I want to. I wanted to lie and say that I was strong enough to give it up, to tuck the experience away in the back of my mind. I wanted to be the kind of person who could resign Zach to something that was once in a lifetime. A mistake that wouldn't be repeated.

There were a lot of things I wanted, and on my way home I tried to convince myself that I could have them all. The truth, of course, was that I knew exactly what would happen the next time I saw Zach. It was as if I'd been starving and now that I'd had my first bite of sustenance, I was trying to stop myself from taking a second. It was nearly impossible and I couldn't help but feel as if the more I struggled against it, the more inevitable it all became.

***

Was it really so wrong to have a few stolen moments of happiness?

When I was in Zach's arms, I couldn't imagine how something that felt so right could be wrong. We met as we usually did, to divert any possible suspicion. Zach was still my emotional counselor and most ardent supporter, but he no longer accepted payment from me for our sessions. While he still gave me advice and was always willing to lend an ear when I needed to vent, our sessions usually ended the same way. Sex had never been this way for me before. Zach didn't make me feel as if my only value lay in my willingness to share my body. While sex with Chris was good, that one small change made all the difference and I found myself responding much more strongly than I had in years.

With Zach things were different. He had years of experience on his side for one, and for another he was used to listening to me. The man knew how to read my unspoken questions when it came to things that I didn't know how to say or perhaps were too shy to ask for. Every time he slipped inside of me, I grew bolder. There was a freedom there, because I didn't have to play games with Zach. I didn't have to smile and fake anything. We were both there for the same reasons: to enjoy one another. That meant that if I wanted something, I demanded it. If I were going to go down this path, I planned on enjoying it and that meant letting my walls down. I did things with Zach I'd never done before, trusted him in ways that I've never trusted a partner before, and my gamble paid off tenfold.

Those hours spent with Zach were precious, addictive in the worst way, but it couldn't last forever. Our time together would invariably end and real life would shove its way back in. I found that when I wasn't around Zach, the warm glow I experienced usually faded into shame. I was always doubting myself, always terrified of being found out. Not enough to make me stop, however. The strange thing is that it was exciting, too. Doing something illicit was a thrill. I knew how to be the good girl, the girl who gave up everything for the sake of everyone else, and I missed those days when life was full of excitement. When every day was new and unpredictable.

Being a wife and mother was amazing. Considering my childhood and my once rocky relationship with my own family, being a housewife was fulfilling. But, it wasn't all I was and unfortunately it took a long time for me to understand that. So many women I knew lost themselves in motherhood; I know because I used to be just like them. I gave up so much of who I was and what I wanted in an attempt to be a 'good' mother that I was identifiable only through my relationship with the people in my life.

I lost myself, and it wasn't until I did so that I understood just how easy that was to do if you weren't being careful. For a while I was so wrapped up in being the perfect mom and wife that I forgot that I used to be anything more than that, that I'd ever aspired for anything more than that.

Some were content with this way of life, but the same things that had once been enough for me now seemed stifling. Repetitive. Doing the same thing day in and day out left me little to look forward to. I never got the chance to disconnect from my position as a wife and just be *Brianna* and every day that passed was like losing a little more of myself. I found Bri, the confident, sexy, happy woman I wanted to be in that office with Zach and the more I got to know her, the more I wanted to see her even outside of our meetings.

I began working out more. It wasn't for Zach's sake so much as it was my own. Exercising made me feel good and seeing the results increased my confidence. I enjoyed the chance to get out of the house for one and the routine gave me more energy once I got used to it. I was not only surprised by the change in my body but by the change in Chris.

After that first time with Zach I'd gone out of my way to avoid him. I still called him on his bullshit, but the desperation I'd once felt to see change had diminished. There had always been the fear that without Chris, I would be alone. It's part of the reason why I put up with so much. I had tasted loneliness and depression and while they were bad, I knew that things could get worse. In fact, it was terrifying to imagine just *how* much worse. But then Zach came along and though I knew intellectually that I shouldn't assign my worth to whether or not someone wanted me, it was hard not to.

I don't want to blame all my insecurities on Chris. At the end of the day I have to take responsibility for the part that I played in things. If I'm being honest, while he may not have been the catalyst, our dynamic and the way he spoke to me certainly didn't help. Even before our relationship took a more intimate turn, Zach couldn't stand him. His dislike for my husband started off small, at first, and grew alongside his frustration as Chris continued to balk at change. On more than one occasion he spoke to me about possibly leaving Chris, but I didn't want to hear it.

He was the father of my kids and despite everything that was going on, despite the things that were said and what was left unsaid, I still loved him. Which made me start to question what exactly it was I felt for Zach. Was it just lust? A crush? Or was there more there? If I weren't married, if I were a different woman, could I say that I loved him? I wasn't sure. The most I knew was that if I weren't married, there would have been the possibility of love between us. But I knew just as well as he did that our relationship had an expiration date. There was no future with him.

On one hand, it was sad but on the other…

On the other it meant that there was nothing holding us back from enjoying one another and that gave me a delicious taste of freedom. Pleasure without strings or expectations. Things I hadn't experienced in so long that I forgot how unencumbered relationships could be. After Chris, I needed something simple. I was no longer as invested in healing our marriage, and I was surprised to note that the same couldn't be said for him. I could tell that he had begun to care in his own way but in many ways, it was too little, too late. Being with Zach was something that consumed not just during our time together but when I was alone as well. I was always thinking about either the last time we saw one another or what it would be like the next time we met. Being fully invested in a relationship outside of my marriage added an extra strain to our already fraying dynamics. For one, now that I was sleeping with Zach, I couldn't in good conscience be intimate with Chris.

A change of affairs that he noticed sooner rather than later. Using the excuse that I was too tired or feeling under the weather worked at first, but they were just that – excuses. Eventually even Chris began to notice that I was growing distant. To be honest, it was a strange sort of poetic justice to be on the other side of the emotional fence for once. It wasn't that I wanted to get back at him or punish him for anything, but I had tried for so long to get him to work with me instead of against me in terms of our marriage that I couldn't help but note the irony once the shoe was on the other foot. The thought occurred to me that now that he understood what it was like to have an emotionally distant partner, maybe he would be less likely to treat me that way in the future. On the other hand, while I would have loved for things to improve, I was starting to consider what life would be like if they didn't. With Zach on my side, I found that I was growing more and more comfortable with the idea.

There was so much guilt that went hand in hand with the happiness, so much confusion. It was almost impossible to navigate the landmine of my marriage while also juggling this huge secret. I wanted to stop but it was like a drug; Zach was the one thing that made me feel good. There were issues of course with our dynamic but they were easy to dismiss or ignore given the circumstances. Sometimes I might feel as if I were the only one making any effort but it wasn't as if I were in any position to talk. All these new feelings and issues often left me depressed. In many ways I was even more unhappy than I'd been before Chris and I had started seeing Zach. That should have been a sign to let him go, but those two or three days of happiness after seeing him were my high and they were enough to keep me coming back for more.

More than once, I would find myself hiding in my room and crying. Sometimes I would just sit on the couch and try my best to feel nothing at all because nothing was better than this overwhelming feeling of being crushed beneath the weight of all that was happening in my life. My new exercise regimen was one of the many changes I made that caught Chris's attention. I needed the distraction in my life and the act of exercising made me feel so good that I started practicing other good habits as well. In those quiet moments to myself, when I was pushing my body to the limit, I would start to fantasize what life would be like without Chris. I realized that in the event that I did leave, I wanted to feel good about myself in the future with someone else. The fantasy was nice but, in the end, it was nothing more than that.

I could tell that Chris was afraid that this new version of me meant that I was on my way out the door however and as time passed, he grew more inclined to show me affection. He even went out of his way to help out around the house more, but I wasn't convinced. The change in him felt hollow, easily broken, and even as I expressed gratitude for the little things he began to do I was waiting for the other shoe to drop and for him to go back to his old ways.

When that happened – as I was convinced that it would – at least I would have a comforting set of arms to turn to. I asked Zach once if he had ever been in my shoes. I think I wanted him to judge me, to make me feel guilty about what we'd done. In those early days perhaps his disapproval would have been enough to turn me away. I had so much respect for him not just as an authority figure, but as a friend. So, I was surprised when he admitted that he'd cheated on his wife on three separate occasions. He said that it was because they had long since stopped having sex. After his divorce, he moved into a one-bedroom apartment and I remember thinking that his choice of living arrangements was a strange one. Considering his line of work, I would have thought that he would have enough money to get a place of his own. Besides that, a one-bedroom apartment left no room for his kids to have a space of their own when they came over to visit. As it was, when they did come by, they would sleep on his bed while he took the couch. In the beginning of his divorce he would spend time at his ex-wife's house; she would make a point of leaving for a while so that he could spend time with them and put them to bed.

His situation raised all sorts of red flags: flags I could ignore during those intimate moments together but which ate at me every second after. Even so, I trusted Zach when he told me that there was nothing to worry about and that he cared about me. I could recognize that he was going through some sort of midlife crisis; after all he was in the middle of a divorce and that would affect anyone. Even so, he always seemed so in control that it never occurred to me that I might be a byproduct of that crisis. Zach was someone who I could take at his word. I needed to believe that, so I did.

Not long after Zach and I became intimate, we found out that an old classmate of mine had died. Natalie was the sister of one of my childhood friends, both of whom my brother was still extremely close with. Even Zach was familiar with her because he'd counseled her for a while. Her memorial service was held at an old middle school and since Zach and I knew that we would both be attending we promised to see each other there despite having to show up separately.

I arrived before he did and paid my condolences, but the entire time I couldn't stop glancing towards the door. Zach and I had agreed on what time we would meet and I was surprised not to see him there sooner, though I shouldn't have been. Zachary had proven time and time again that he did things in his own time and the rest of the world had to readjust accordingly. The thought should have been one of those things that dissipated as soon as it showed its face, but for some reason I fixated on the idea.

Since our relationship had shifted, I was always the one waiting for him. Everything we did was on his time. I turned the thought over in my mind for several minutes, trying to find loopholes or an exception that I could point to that would undermine my theory. But there was nothing. When it came to our communication, I was always the one reaching out and left twisting in the wind until he had time to talk to me. In fact, I often got the impression that his correspondences were designed to appease me when I grew too insistent on an equal give-and-take. As if he measured out his affection with the intent of only giving me enough to keep me around.

I wasn't sure where these thoughts came from, but it happened frequently. When we weren't together, my mind raced and questions surfaced. That's just how it went and I had no way of stopping the doubts from crowding in and weighing me down. In the moment it seemed as if I was finally thinking clearly, but once I was in his arms again, I felt silly and paranoid. When Zach kissed me, I knew that I was sexy, wanted. I desperately wanted to carry that confidence and sense of self-worth over into every aspect of my life, but it was hard. Especially with things at home spiraling out of my control.

I was smart enough to realize that I was already in too deep; Zach had my complete attention, and in a way I think he thrived on it. As soon as this all occurred to me, I rationalized it. After all, he couldn't exactly reach out as much as I would like him to. I was the one with the family. It made sense that I should be the one to determine the pacing of our communication. That's what I told myself, but there was still a kernel of discontent I simply couldn't shake.

The door to the auditorium opened and I turned instinctively to watch the new guests enter. I held my breath until I caught a glimpse of Zach. My heart leapt and when Zach winked at me my nervousness ratcheted up another notch. Not only were we out in public, we were surrounded by people we both knew. Though nothing had happened, I couldn't help but imagine that everyone who looked at us could tell. As if there was a visible thread tying the two of us together. That wink might as well have been a declaration of ownership as far as I was concerned. Yet an anxious glance around confirmed that no one had noticed. Knowing that the paranoia was all in my head, I continued to smile and nod at the conversation I was having with one of my old acquaintances as Zach made his rounds.

He hugged everyone he spoke to so by the time he got to me and wrapped his arms around my waist, the embrace seemed just par for the course. I sunk into his arms, hugging him tight and luxuriating in his now familiar warmth and scent. Despite the situation my body still reacted to his touch as if we were alone. I shied away from catching his eye, stomach in knots. It was enviable, the way he was able to interact with everyone as if there was nothing at all between us. I wished I could be as cool under pressure. Maybe if I could camouflage my own emotions just as well life would be easier.

It took several minutes but Zach and I were finally able to get a second alone. Reaching out he gripped my hand in his as if he were offering comfort and I shifted, lowering my voice so I wouldn't be overheard.

"Are you coming to the bar later?"

Several of us had agreed to head over to a nearby bar for drinks to unwind and to continue the celebration of her life.

His brows shot up and he smiled slightly. "I might, if I had some incentive."

I shivered; already I was tightening, ready for something more. Ready to explore the promise only I could hear in his voice.

"I'm sure I could think of something," I assured him.

"I'm sure you could." Zach angled his head to one side, studying me. "In fact, let's leave a little early. I want some time alone with you before we have to perform for the masses."

I bit my lip and nodded, momentarily unable to speak. In the end all I could say was "I would like that." It was an understatement of course. We never went out together and the promise of spending time with him out in such an obvious setting was like a dream. The term 'friends with benefits' had been thrown around several times now, though we'd only been intimate twice. It shouldn't have bothered me. We weren't a couple, of course, but that didn't change how I felt. Some people could have sex and keep their emotions out of it but I had never been one of them. What I did feel for Zach was already complex before we started sleeping together. Now that we were intimate, it had only gotten worse. I tried to enjoy it all for what it was, but I couldn't help but want more. Emotionally, I was already dependent on him and now that things had crossed the line into something physical, I couldn't keep those softer, more permanent emotions from creeping in.

It made sense then that going to the bar felt a lot like going on a date and I was as jittery as I'd been the first time a boy had asked me out. We agreed to a time and I spent the next hour trying desperately not to watch the clock and failing. When the appointed time came around, I was so amped that I had to struggle to remain casual so as not to arouse suspicion when I snuck out. The bar itself was only a few blocks away; my brother and I rode to the service together and since he was going to pick up a few friends afterward, I asked him if he could just go ahead and drop me off at the bar on his way. When I arrived, I found a seat where I could see the door. Soon enough, our secret rendezvous became another waiting game. I kept checking the clock, growing increasingly nervous the later it got. Soon, the other guests from the memorial would arrive and Zach and I would miss our opportunity. I shifted uncomfortably, already growing upset by the time my phone finally rang.

"Where are you?"

In the background I could hear the sounds of people talking and the soft melody of music. He was still at the memorial and my lips tightened with disappointment.

"Sorry," he began, "I got caught up talking to everyone so I won't make it."

"Oh." It was a struggle to keep my voice even but somehow, I managed it. "That's fine." As I spoke the door opened and several of my old classmates came in, already deep in conversation. "You know what? Everyone else is already here anyway, so I'll just see you later."

I got off the phone before I could say anything else, just in time to smile in welcome when everyone else spotted me. I wasn't sure if Zach was still going to come and I tried not to think too hard about it either way. Thinking about him at all was a distraction I didn't need at the moment. Luckily everyone attributed any strange behavior on my part to the loss of Natalie. Though sad, the two of us hadn't been close. It hurt that she was gone, but it was a distant sort of hurt, not nearly strong enough to outweigh what was already on my mind. When Zach finally strolled in, I very carefully avoided eye contact. Because I wanted to do the exact opposite, I decided that it was even more important to give Zach his space. If I were important, he would make the time to be with me. It was something that he himself had been preaching during our sessions about Chris.

'If he cared, he would make the effort to be there.'

Still, I was secretly pleased when he made a point to sit next to me. Conversation ebbed and flowed around us and I got the distinct impression that we were hanging out, but not really. We shared a silent knowledge, an invisible connection, that only the two of us could feel. It was like sharing an inside joke with your best friend; the slightest touch, the briefest glance, was all it took for warmth to blossom in the middle of my chest. I didn't like being stood up, but that disappointment seemed distant and silly now.

The longer we sat and drank, the more comfortable I became. What had begun as a somber affair quickly turned into a celebration. Many of us hadn't seen one another in years and the impromptu reunion lightened all of our spirits. I especially needed a night out; it felt good to be away from Chris for a couple of hours. It was also nice to have a break from the kids for a while. They were precious, but they were also a handful and I needed some time to just be. Not a mom or a wife, just…be. Surrounded by people I knew, with Zach by my side I was reminded that I used to have a life outside of my house. That I used to have interests and hobbies that didn't revolve around taking care of my family or struggling to preserve my marriage.

For a little while, I allowed myself to forget and I'll admit, once I made the decision to let go, I grew extra flirtatious. It was so difficult to have all of these feelings fighting for dominance within me and not be able to express any of them. I liked to think that I played it cool, but there was no way to tell for sure. Whatever I did must have worked however because Zach caught my attention and smirked.

"Go for a walk with me?"

His voice against the shell of my ear was a shock and a shiver went down my spine. I nodded mutely. Everyone else was already a few drinks in and talking loudly. It was nothing for one of us to get up and leave and the other to follow a few moments later. We met outside and I reached for his hand, feeling daring with the shadows wrapped tight around us and curious eyes a thing of the past. With the stars shining above our heads, the world seemed to slow and for a moment I was dazzled by the sight of my breath hanging in the air. We picked our way carefully down the sidewalk side by side, keeping a sharp eye out for any ice the salt might have missed. I could almost pretend that we were just normal lovers. That there was nothing holding us back from laying claim to something more. I wanted that — not to lose my family but to gain something intangible. Something I'd thought I'd found once with Chris.

The connection between Zach and I felt too good to be true, but between the two of us our combined baggage meant that we were too fucked up to ever be a reality. Even so, I remained ever hopeful that we could have something real, though I wasn't in a position to ask for such a thing. My fingers tightened around his and I bit my lip. It was often hard to ignore my unease about what we were doing when my thoughts weren't clouded with lust. Our relationship went against everything I believed in, yet I had grown used to ignoring my own gut. As a result, I searched for reassurance any way that I could, hoping to unearth his true intentions without coming across as clingy.

I would tease him about being that creepy old guy on the prowl for his next bit of arm candy and Zach would assure me that it was possible for a 'guy like him' to be interested in me. It wasn't a declaration of love, but he had a way of making me feel confident. Every text or call when we weren't together brightened my day and helped me get through the rough nights, fighting with Chris, and those endless days that were becoming increasingly unbearable.

So it was little wonder that something as simple as a walk could inspire such contentment within me. I was overjoyed, even grateful that he would show me so much attention with so many people we both knew around. It was the first time we were seeing one another outside of his office and I'd been afraid that he would ignore me once we were susceptible to public scrutiny. Somehow we ended up at his car, a black Acura SUV. It was a relief to get out of the cold. It was December in Illinois and the chill in the air was enough to make your bones ache.

We smoked for a few minutes, reminiscing about the past and sharing a few laughs. The longer I sat next to him, the hotter my blood grew. I felt as if I were balancing on a knife's edge. My body knew the kind of pleasure he could offer me and wanted more of it. When I couldn't take it anymore, I reached out and grabbed his face, pulling him towards me and kissing him with all of the passion I could muster. His tongue tasted like the vodka from the Dirty Shirley he'd been drinking and I grew drunk off the dark ecstasy hidden there. Any discontent I may have felt over the course of the night had long since dissipated like smoke.

Like always, the rest of the world disappeared whenever he kissed me. I forgot where we were and why, too wrapped up in his touch to know up from down or right from wrong. One palm held the side of my face while the other traveled lower, cupping my breast until I arched into his hand. We lost ourselves in one another and I liked to think that Zach found as much peace in my arms as I did in his. This was what kept bringing me back again and again, this was what made those dark days of guilt, fear, and uncertainty worth it. I belonged right here with the one man who understood me the best.

We lingered there for as long as we could, but all too soon had to return to the bar. The time had already gotten away from us and we practically jogged down the sidewalk in the hopes of getting back before anyone noticed that we were gone. I felt like a teenager again, flush with possibility and the butterflies that accompanied a first love. I didn't like using that word so soon, even in my thoughts, because it was such a slippery slope to find myself on. Yet how else could I describe the sensation growing in the pit of my stomach and this need that occupied my every waking moment? Just the smell of his cologne or the sound of his voice was enough to loosen the knots in my gut that Chris often left there.

I didn't want this to be love, but it didn't seem as if I had much of a choice in the matter.

Chapter Nine

"Where'd you wander off to?"

If I were a cat I would have leapt a foot off the ground. We were back in the bar and I was trying to decide if I was ready to go home or not. Most of our group was dissipating so it wouldn't be weird if I left now as well. Conversation had been winding down for some time, so I was surprised when my longtime friend Clarissa sat beside me as if settling in for a long talk.

"What do you mean?"

She made a face and took a sip of her drink. "You know what I mean," she smirked. "I saw you and Mr. Harris sneak off together earlier." She laughed. "Don't tell me he's working off the clock now. Talk about dedication." Her brows furrowed with concern. "How's the counseling going by the way?"

There it was.

I'd always wondered how I would react if and when someone finally saw the two of us together. While Clarissa didn't seem to suspect anything, the fact that she had seen us walking off together left me uncomfortable. It would be all too easy to put two and two together. Leaning back in my seat I tried to affect a casual air, but even I could hear how strained I sounded.

"Great." My chest was tight and it was hard to draw in a breath. "He just…wanted to check on me, you know?"

Clarissa seemed to be expecting something more. Maybe she wanted me to tell her how Chris and I were doing now that Zach was working with us. I didn't bother expounding, however. Given the situation, I couldn't exactly afford to start thinking about Chris right now. That was a surefire way to undermine my composure. My greatest fear was that Clare had seen the two of us making out. God, why hadn't we gone somewhere more private? Or further away? Anyone walking by could have seen us and we had been so distracted that we wouldn't even have noticed.

Clare made a face, eyeing me suspiciously for a moment while my heart beat so fast I was sure I was about to have a heart attack. "That's good." Her brow furrowed and after a moment of thought she shook her head in amusement. "For a while it sounded like the two of you were flirting or something."

I laughed nervously and my voice was pitched high with nerves. Too high. I probably sounded like a crazy person. My mind raced, scrambling to come up with something simple, something plausible. I hated lying. It was something I wasn't good at and would likely never get used to. "That's probably my fault. I have a little crush on him," I admitted quickly. "Dr. Harris has been extremely patient with me about the whole thing and we just stepped outside to talk a bit about Natalie."

Clare didn't seem all that convinced, but she let it go.

We talked for a while longer before I was finally able to pull myself away. It was around then that I realized that I'd had too much to drink throughout the course of the night. Likely driven by a mixture of excitement and nervous energy. Zach must have noticed as much because he went to order me an Uber while I sat down for a while. By then it was too late however, because I had called Chris to come and pick me up and he was already on his way. While I waited for him to arrive, I couldn't help but think about what a disaster the night had almost turned out to be. Zach and I had to be more careful. This was the only time we'd been out and we'd almost been found out. What if someone had come outside to check on one or the both of us? Clearly our exit hadn't been as clandestine as we'd thought. Clare may not have been the only one to notice us leaving together or the way we bantered back and forth. It was like stepping into a nightmare. My biggest worry had been that someone could tell what was going on between us simply by looking and listening, and it was true. It didn't help that everyone knew us, at least if we'd been out with strangers I would have felt less exposed, less vulnerable to attack.

I went home, fully expected Chris to call me out on what I'd been doing and with whom. Already I was convinced that word had spread, that maybe Clare had reached out to him on Facebook or spoken to a mutual acquaintance of ours. I was so nervous, anyone looking at me would have thought that I was waiting for a SWAT team to kick down my door and lead me away in handcuffs.

In fact, that sounded like a walk in the park compared to what I was really afraid of. It was almost a relief to simply go about my night as usual. The next day passed in much the same way that it always did. With every hour that ticked by with nothing happening, I grew more convinced that Clare had bought my story. It should have been a relief. It *was* a relief; though I couldn't help but wonder how long I could keep up the charade. Going through life constantly feeling as if there was a pendulum swinging overhead, agonizing over when that first blow would fall, always on edge; it was enough to drive me crazy.

For some crazy reason, Zach was the first person I thought to turn to. Talking to him always made me feel better, even if he was the reason for my current situation. It still seemed surreal that this person, this man that I regarded so highly, knew all my weaknesses and yet still wanted to give me his time and attention. Even with what he had going on in his personal life, I counted myself lucky to be considered one of his priorities. I kept telling myself that there was no way he could see anything in me, but he always managed to put my doubts to rest. A few long phone calls and casual texts riddled with smiley faces and the occasional heart emoji was all it took to hold me over until I got to see him again the following month.

***

The first time we hung out, just the two of us, was something I planned very carefully for. Even going so far as to splurge on a new outfit after finding my own wardrobe painfully lacking. It wasn't like we were going to a five-star restaurant; it was the simple fact that we were going out to a public venue in the first place that made the occasion so special. I tried not to psych myself out about it, but it was all I could think about once we agreed on where and when to meet.

We decided on a restaurant in downtown Naperville. Usually we sat in his office whenever we were together. It was the only place we knew for sure where we wouldn't be recognized by anyone that we knew. Meeting up beyond the privacy of those four walls was a risk, but nothing that couldn't be explained so long as we kept things casual. Which is exactly what we did, even though I longed to hold his hand or press a kiss to his lips. Though the moment lacked some

147

of the intimacy that usually accompanied our rendezvous within his office, it made up for it in other ways.

Even with all those eyes and voices surrounding us, or rather, especially because of those things, there was a delicious normalcy to the encounter that wasn't lost on me. It should have been uncomfortable, the fear that at any moment someone one of us might know would walk past and start asking questions, start connecting dots, and at first it was. But the more time that passed, the easier it got. My nervousness faded along with the last of my defenses and I realized that I was being silly. Zach and I had already gone over the pros and cons of being seen together and they were minuscule. If there was any chance of our tête-à-tête being seen as anything other than innocent, Zach would never have risked it.

It was strange, but I had more to lose than Zach and yet he seemed to be the more reluctant of the two of us to initiate things. He could always find a new job, make a new start for himself, but if our relationship came to light then I stood to lose my entire family. They were irreplaceable and I often found myself battling down a surge of frustration when it felt as if I were putting more effort into what we had than he was. In some ways, it reminded me a lot of my dynamic with Chris in which I was often the one striving to keep things going. I placated myself with the knowledge that even with the twenty-year age difference, what Zach and I shared was nothing like what I had with Chris.

Yet, I craved more.

It wasn't in me *not* to crave more. I *always* wanted more. Sometimes my heart seemed like a cup that would never know what it was to be full. I wondered sometimes if it was because there was a crack in the glass itself or the men I hoped would quench my thirst were running on empty themselves.

Strangely, it seemed like the closer Zach and I grew, the less we saw one another. Or maybe it was because the time we spent apart grew harder to handle. The weeks in between our meetings grew painful, to the point where I struggled to distract myself anyway that I knew how until I could see Zach again. It was difficult not to feel like a hypocrite; I wanted more but had no right to ask for it. While there was an obvious solution to my dilemma, I wasn't yet ready to consider divorce *or* stop things with Zach. While my feelings for Chris were changing, I didn't want to make such a permanent decision when I didn't even know what I wanted. I needed to know what was happening between Zach and me, but we saw one another so rarely that it was impossible to tell for sure. My hope was that I would gain clarity the more I was with him, which is why I took our time together so seriously.

Despite my many reservations, I wanted to put myself out there when it came to Zach. I wanted him to want me with the same passion that I felt towards him. It was a constant thing, seeking reassurances that he was with me because his desire to be there equaled my own, but he always managed to say the right thing. To reassure and appease.

That's what it felt like.

Being appeased.

Almost as if he didn't truly mean the words, he just knew what to say and when. Deep down, I didn't believe him. Maybe that's why I always needed to hear the platitudes. Still, I wanted to believe him at face value, so that's exactly what I strove to do. And why not? Things had already gone so far that there was little else that I had to lose by putting my faith in him. In fact, it wasn't until we met again for lunch at a restaurant in Elburn – both crossing our fingers that we wouldn't see anyone we knew in a town so small that everyone seemed to know everyone else – that I realized something.

It was my trust in him that had me hooked.

Being with Zach was new and exciting and I couldn't bring myself to give that up even though the consequences of continuing with our relationship were always lurking at the back of my mind. I kept telling myself that this was Zach. The person I could count on to always have my back. I believed that whatever was happening between us was happening for a reason, that it was just that important, because surely Zach wouldn't put me through this stress for something casual and meaningless. He wasn't the kind of person who would put me in a situation that would make things worse for me and that left me feeling safe and secure when I was anything but.

***

Sitting across from Zach as we had lunch and talked about trivial things always made my chest ache with longing. Those moments were what I wanted for myself – what I wanted for us. I craved that attention, the high from having real conversations with someone that I admired. I was hungry for someone to want me and when we met up, especially when it was outside of his office, it was easy to pretend that this was all there was. That there were no obligations and broken promises waiting for me back home. Zach taught me what it was to live in the moment. To enjoy someone fully for as long as we were together and let the worries of the past go.

A philosophy that was great in the moment, but something I seemed to struggle with once he was out of sight. His was a concept I struggled to accept and only added to my confusion about everything. I tried to apply his words to my everyday life, but couldn't. Mainly because it didn't make sense to me that he could behave one way when I was with him and then act so differently when I wasn't around.

For all the great things that came with it, being with him also had its downsides.

For one, I was never truly convinced about his sincerity. Somewhere along the way I managed to convince myself that as long as he was still reaching out to me then that must mean that he wanted to spend time with me. I hoped that one day, the last of his reticence would fade and we would get to see one another more often. But no matter how hopeful I was, nothing ever changed. The waits between the moments we saw one another left me feeling as if I'd lost a piece of myself.

"You know," I would tell him, "the way you make me feel when we're together actually makes all the pain in between worth it." I tried to smile, but it was hard knowing that our time would be up soon and I would have to leave again. "I'm willing to suffer a little if it means I get to have you in my life."

I expressed this same sentiment on more than one occasion. Sometimes he would laugh it off, other times he would reassure me, and still there were times when he said and did nothing at all. I got the impression that Zach was seeing someone. Either that or he just wasn't as interested anymore. While he knew how to make me feel better about my suspicions in the heat of the moment, there was still something vital missing.

For all my hope, I wasn't naïve. Our relationship wouldn't last forever. I tried to tell myself that while the day would come where we could no longer share the same intimacy that I had grown used to, but it wasn't all bad. After all, at the time I was sure that he would forever be a part of my life. Zach didn't want anything serious, and knowing that his intentions were pure and that he wasn't seeing anyone else bought me time to figure out what *I* wanted and who I ultimately saw myself spending my life with. Plus, if we were together – even if we weren't pursuing something permanent yet – that meant that he wasn't out searching for someone more available.

Our situation was a unique one because despite our level of physical intimacy, Zach would always encourage me to go out and meet guys, to put myself out there. He would treat me as if I were single and I would always have to remind him that I wasn't in a position to take his advice. We spoke openly about so many things, including Chris or Zach's latest date, but there was no denying the connection we had with one another in spite of these outside influences.

Though it seemed – and felt – irrational considering the circumstances, I lived in fear of the day that Zach would replace me. I was constantly comparing myself to other women: *single* women.

That one was better looking than I was, the one over there was more successful, the blonde at the red light looked like she might be around his age – they'd probably have a lot more in common.

To be clear, I wasn't nervous about Zach having a physical relationship with someone else. He could date around all he wanted because what the two of us had was special. He'd told me so, and I had grown accustomed to finding what I believed to be traces of love in the small acts of care he deigned to gift me with. Chris hadn't changed at all during this time and Zach told me that instead of wasting my time going in circles with someone who refused to budge, I should focus more on myself. That it would be more beneficial for me in the long run. There was no denying that he had a point and once I was no longer as focused on saving my marriage, I spent more time practicing self-care and working on myself. It was one of the few distractions I had besides the kids. I found joy in running, lost the forty pounds I gained while I was pregnant, and learned how to be more opinionated and assertive. When all was said and done, these changes gave me a major confidence boost and I attributed these positive changes to this idea that it was all proof that Zach was good for me.

I could see myself becoming the woman I'd wanted to be for so long, I no longer felt stagnant and lost as I had for so long with Chris; surely that meant that no matter how bad things might seem between Zach and me sometimes or how sad I might feel, something must be going right.

That was yet one more reason why I couldn't move forward and make a decision; being with Zach made me want to be a better woman. I was more motivated than I'd been in years. But was this newfound change only because I was lonely? Or did he simply bring out the best in me? It was impossible to tell when our relationship was relegated to only a few hours a month with text messages and phone calls scattered across the interim. While what we had was important to me, I couldn't tell if it was worth leaving Chris for. If I were just confused and unhappy, then leaving my husband and unraveling the life we'd built together could be the biggest mistake I'd ever made. I wanted desperately to love Chris the way that I used to, to look at him and see the man I'd once promised my loyalty to. But I couldn't because Zach was always there in my mind and heart, distracting me.

Had I fallen out of love with my husband or was it just because Zach was there when I found myself in an emotionally vulnerable place? I didn't like to think of the possibility that he had taken advantage of his position and my situation, but in my darkest moments it was impossible not to acknowledge that it's exactly what he'd done.

After that first day, there were numerous more lunch 'dates' that followed. Each was a revelation because it gave Zach the platform he needed to confide in me. The more he opened up, the more convinced I became that what we had went deeper than the occasional bout of lovemaking. We bonded not only over mutual acquaintances, but we would update one another on our day-to-day lives as well. I would tell him about the people in my life and what they were up to and he would offer up his opinion, even returning the favor a time or two and telling me about individuals I'd never met before. We talked about our kids and discussed our beliefs on parenting and relationships, about our favorite books or recent documentaries he'd seen.

The conversation was always easy, flowing as if we'd been a constant in each other's lives for decades rather than months. On one hand I wondered if he was so easy to talk to because of his profession. He could interact with anyone, he had been trained to do just that. I'd seen the proof of it when Chris and I had first begun our sessions with him. It had only taken a few minutes before Zach and my husband were chatting like old friends and Chris was notoriously tight-lipped. So much so that he could come across as antisocial or even egotistical depending on his mood at the time. But surely if Zach were just stringing me along, he wouldn't reveal such personal information about himself. I knew how much his divorce and the resulting custody battles affected his life and how concerned he was about being a good father and being there for his kids. On top of that Zach studied journalism before he got into therapy, which had been my major in college so we shared a mutual love of words and storytelling.

For someone who knew how to get people to let down their guard without revealing any personal information about himself, he was an open book to me. I felt special knowing that I was one of the few he let in and could trust. It just seemed like every time he did something to make me feel special, something happened to throw a shadow over my contentment. One incident in particular stood out for me. We were supposed to meet at Bar Louie for lunch, and Zach stood me up. This wasn't the first time he claimed to be too busy to make time for me. Sometimes he simply brushed it off as something that slipped his mind. On this occasion he said that he had forgotten that he had another client coming in shortly after his previous one and that we could have lunch in between his appointments. Suggesting that I order some food and bring it to his office if I wanted to see him.

That day I had made an extra effort, from my hair and makeup to my clothes. I'd gone out of my way to make time to see and talk to him and while he noticed me going that extra mile, he was never inclined to do the same. They say that no matter how busy someone is, a person will make time and room for what they consider important. It often seemed as if Zach was only reaching out in order to keep me around and not because he actually missed me, and despite all of our conversations about our relationship and our feelings for one another I couldn't help but realize that he was never clear on what he wanted from me. Though we didn't always have sex when we saw one another, he had a habit of treating our meetings like hookups.

Which was to say that when we were together, he gave me his all. And when we weren't, it was as if I'd fallen in love with a ghost. Like a ghost, our affair haunted me even if Zach wasn't always around to take the blame. It was around this time that I learned that Rachel had taken the liberty of reaching out to Zach without consulting me. After revealing to her that he returned my feelings back in November, she grew concerned enough to write to him, threatening repercussions for breaking doctor/patient boundaries. Of course, Zach called me out about it, explaining that what was going on between us was special and that no one else would understand if they knew. After that, I no longer had the urge to confide in my friends about the latest change in my life.

The incident taught me a valuable lesson. If I was going to do this, I couldn't go about it half-assed. We'd almost gotten caught once before and now Rachel was asking questions that could cost Zach his practice. Her concern, while valid, was irritating at the time. She had such a strong opinion about what was going on, but I didn't want to hear it because I was determined to explore whatever it was between us. I didn't want anything getting in the way of that and I didn't want to drag anyone else into this whole sordid mess, not only because it wouldn't have been fair to ask Rachel to lie to Chris – who she considered a friend – but also because I didn't want the truth coming out when I was still torn about what to do with the two men in my life. I didn't want circumstances to make a decision for me. I didn't want to be forced into either leaving Chris or dumping Zach because of a slipup that somehow spiraled out of my control.

In the end, it was easier and safer to distance myself from my friends so I wouldn't run the risk of getting Zach into any trouble. I couldn't confide in them about what was going on and I was juggling so many lies already when it came to Chris that I didn't have it in me to lie to anybody else. I told myself that it was for the best, but the more I pulled away from the people in my life, the larger Zach's presence loomed. He became both the source of my isolation and the only cure for it.

Tiffany revealed herself to be an unexpected ally. If it wasn't for her, there's a chance I might have gone crazy during the days and weeks that passed in between seeing Zach. Our meetings had gone from once a week to once a month with long stretches of silence in between. It gave me too much time to think and desperate for company, I sometimes went against my better judgment and reached out to some of the people in my life for advice.

My brother was one and Tiffany was another.

Revealing my secret to my brother, Michael, was one thing. He and Zach knew one another. I hadn't been the only one to see Zach for counseling back in high school and telling him about the affair seemed only natural. Michael was a regular confidant and the two of us had a good relationship, so it was just one of those things.

Opening up to Tiffany was both just as easy and ten times harder than talking to Michael. I thought that if anyone could inspire me towards one direction or another, it would be the woman who I considered to be the embodiment of marital bliss. The two of us had been friends for a long time and I was already keeping so much from so many people that I was curious to see if she was someone I could rely on with this information. A part of me was afraid that she would judge, so at first, I only confided in her about having a 'crush' on Zach – just to see how she would respond. It was a shock to learn that Tiffany's marriage wasn't the Hallmark movie I'd always envisioned it as.

"Funny you should say that," she said, and I couldn't help but notice that she didn't seem all that amused. "There's actually something I wanted to talk to you about."

I don't know what I expected her to say, but a hushed admission about her own affair wasn't it. As it turned out, Tiffany was starting to have feelings for one of her coworkers and I could tell that she was just as eager to have someone to talk to about it as I was. It took a while for me to accept and deep down, I still didn't fully believe it until I saw the two of them together. My mental image of Tiffany wouldn't coincide with the reality of what she was telling me. I was so used to thinking of her life as perfect, as a model to live up to, and here we both were doing the exact same thing.

While I wasn't the only one having an affair, the difference between Tiffany and me was that she seemed to revel in her misdemeanors as much as I agonized over mine. The two of us grew closer because we shared the same sin, and more often than not I found myself acting as camouflage for her indiscretions. I wanted to be a good friend and be there for her. I understood better than anyone just how alone she must have felt and I was determined to relieve some of that pressure she was under. It's what I would have wanted someone to do for me. Though I could admit that Tiffany began taking liberties that I wasn't altogether comfortable with. She would tell her husband that she was with me when she wasn't or come over to my house to meet her lover when she had nowhere else to go. This compounded the guilt I was already battling with since Chris and I were friends with both Tiffany *and* her husband.

I knew that if he ever found out about the part I was playing that it would ruin our relationship and destroy any respect he had for me. Unfortunately, I didn't have it in me to stand up for myself when she put me in certain situations, especially when those situations involved being an alibi for her affair. Inevitably there were times where I hung out with her and her coworker so I was very much an accomplice to the web she was weaving. Besides all of that, there were times that I needed her to cover for me in return and I felt that I couldn't say anything about what she was doing without sounding like a hypocrite. I saw a bit of myself in her – and, though the things she asked of me sometimes left me uncomfortable, I liked seeing her happy because it reminded me of the way Zach made me feel. I looked up to her and stupidly found myself justifying my actions because we were both in the same boat. Reasoning that if someone like her – a woman with a big heart and strong morals – was having an affair then surely it wasn't such a harsh mark against my character for being in the same situation.

It didn't seem fair to judge her for what she was doing, but the added pressure of hiding both her affair as well as my own soon took its toll. The both of us were so mired in our own lies as well as each other's that I'm sure she felt the pressure as much as I did. There was no one with whom I didn't have to hide some version of the truth from except Zach. Yet as the months ticked by, I couldn't shake the suspicion that he had secrets of his own that he was all too willing to keep from me.

Chapter Ten

It was always a question of 'when' he would break my heart, not 'if.'

I knew that if I could just learn more about this person who I believed cared for me, that I would feel better. But no matter how much Zach opened up, there was still this invisible wall between us. Egging on my insecurities as soon as I thought myself cured of them. Sometimes I wouldn't hear from him for days and weeks at a time, and my anxiety that he was going to simply vanish on me one day ratcheted up another notch. Zach had taught me to confide in him, regardless of how embarrassing, so I never shied away from expressing how I felt. How not knowing what was going on was fodder for every doubt and fear in my mind. Zach never allowed my doubts about his intentions or actions to last for very long. He was always eager to reassure me that he would never hurt me or disappear from my life.

While we may not have seen one another as much as I would have liked, those moments we did have together left me on top of the world. The next time I was in his office, we sat together on the small couch and talked. I crossed my legs over his and soon talking devolved into kissing, and kissing grew into something more. I took him into my mouth, luxuriating in the guttural sounds he made as I laved my tongue over flesh.

This was power, I knew. It didn't matter if he ignored me or dated someone else. When I had him beneath me, in my hands, filling my mouth, *I* was the one who held all of the cards. I was used to being timid in my everyday life, used to questioning so much, that when I was with him the urge to push past my comfort zone and take control was overwhelming. That day, as I mounted him, hips rising and falling, gasping softly against his ear as the sensation of him moving inside of me left my mind blank with pleasure, I knew that I would put up with anything for moments like this.

Staring out the window through his sheer white curtains, I wondered if the people milling outside along busy Washington Street could see us. What would they think if they could? Imagining their shock made me giggle and Zach hushed me, his warnings that I was being too loud only adding to my sudden bout of lighthearted amusement.

He left with a hug that warmed me down to my core and a chaste kiss on the forehead. Back at home, I awoke the next morning with a silly text message and a link to the music video "Safe Travels" by Lisa Hannigan. That day, I spent hours trying to decode a possible hidden message in the song. Did it mean anything? Was he saying that he cared for me? Or was it just another reminder that things couldn't be between us? Despite agonizing over the lyrics, nothing could have wiped the smile from my face. That's how he always managed to reel me back in. By making me forget what the world was like when he wasn't in it with me. Everything seemed so genuine, so mutual, when he treated me that way. So why wasn't he as eager to increase our time together as I was? It wasn't as if I wanted to be around him 24/7, but Zach was against even calling or texting me more often.

If I were anyone else – Tiffany perhaps – his reticence would have been perfect. I wasn't in a position to give or receive more from him and Zach blamed his lack of attention on his work and his custody schedule.

"Between my clients and my kids I barely have time for myself these days, let alone a relationship. Pretending otherwise wouldn't be fair to either of us. You know that, right?"

Of course I did. It's why I promised not to be too expectant of his time until his schedule freed up. That didn't mean that the radio silence didn't hurt in the meantime, however, and I found myself sending lengthy texts expressing how I felt and begging him to be honest with me when the time came that he no longer reciprocated my feelings. I needed him to be up front when it came time to end things because anything else would break me.

"Don't be silly," he would say. "You know how special you are to me. When are you free next week?"

And on, and on, it went.

***

April 20, 2017, was the first time I went to his apartment.

The drive there seemed to last forever, mostly thanks to nerves though the bumper-to-bumper traffic certainly didn't help. What was supposed to have been a forty-five-minute drive took nearly an hour; I drove past unfamiliar landmarks, relying almost entirely on Google Maps to help me find my way. While Zach and I had been intimate a few times by now and sometimes saw one another for lunch, my stomach twisted nervously at the thought of stepping foot inside of his home. The office, some random restaurant or bar, those were all safe zones.

Neutral territory.

His apartment was different. There he would be the one in control, the one in his element surrounded by the familiar. I trusted him, I did, but I couldn't help but wonder what kind of difference that would make. Sex wasn't in my plans for the evening, but I knew that the possibility was definitely there. I was already having such a hard time separating thoughts of him from the other parts of my life and I didn't want this visit to make it any worse. What would it be like to make love with him in his bedroom, surrounded by the scent of him? To see him padding barefoot through his kitchen? To enter his space and know that it was an intimacy that he allowed few others?

If I were smart, I would have turned around and gone home but the desire to see him vulnerable and in his natural habitat was too great to ignore. I wanted this visit to be the thing that finally tore down the last of the walls between us, and yet I feared what might be lying on the other side and how it might change things between us.

Sitting in the parking garage, I had an uncomfortable moment of déjà vu. It reminded me so strongly of the first time I'd gone to his office after confessing my feeling that it brought a smile to my face. I was being silly. There was nothing to worry about here. This was what I'd been waiting for, Zach to let me in in some tangible way. What was more tangible than going to the man's house?

The pep talk was enough to get me out of the car, carrying me through the parking garage and towards his apartment building. But with every step I took, uncertainty dogged my heels. It was a relief to look up and find him waiting for me at the entrance, a bright grin on his face. He was a familiar, welcome presence, in what had become a day full of uncertainty.

Pulling open a set of heavy glass doors, he studied me with open affection. Already I was noticing a difference. He was more open here, more prone to give me a peek beneath the mask he wore in public and even at work oftentimes.

I liked it.

"I'm glad you could make it."

Not sure what to say, I nodded.

"Did you have any trouble finding the place?"

I laughed, surprised. "I actually would have been here sooner if people knew how to drive."

"Ah," he said, leading me towards the elevator. "In that case I'm shocked you found me at all."

Banter was good.

Banter kept me from turning and making a run for it back to my car. Why was this so stressful? I've seen the man naked. Setting foot inside of his apartment should have been a breeze after that. You would think that once you knew what someone's penis looked like, there would no longer be any need for an icebreaker but apparently not.

As soon as the elevator doors closed, the conversation between us died and was replaced by something else. Something hungry and familiar. The outside world shut its eyes and Zach gripped me, pinning me against the wall and pressing his lips to mine. There it was again. That look beneath the surface that I had only seen glimpses of before. Even the way he kissed me was different. There was an aggression, a passion, a heat that I never got to explore during the timed meetings that had defined our relationship thus far. Here, there was no clock counting down the seconds until I had to get dressed and pretend as if I'd never felt his touch.

I could stay as long as I wanted, be as loud as I wanted, and not a soul would care.

It struck me then, why coming here was so nerve-racking. Because being with Zach like this left me without the armor of being a married woman. I'd never thought of it that way before, as armor. Up until now it had just been a weight. A source of guilt and frustration. These days, thoughts of my marriage made me feel like a bird trapped in a cage for far too long. I was never sure if I would soar once that door was open or find myself unwilling to make that leap for fear of losing the familiar. The safe.

It wasn't until I found myself panting beneath Zach's touch that I realized that there was so much more to it. Being married gave me a level of protection that I had never consciously considered.

It was impossible to commit fully to Zach because I was married.

If I couldn't commit then there was still a cushion between him and my heart. It wouldn't protect me completely, but it kept me wary of his affection. Kept me on my toes. Allowed me to question those weeks of silence, to call bullshit on his declarations of loyalty and love. He could never truly, deeply, hurt me because I could never be his – not truly. Not deeply. Not so long as I had a ring on my finger. In that regard, it was a safety net for my emotions that I desperately needed. I could leave his office knowing full well that he was likely seeing other people, I could pretend that we were just acquaintances when we were seen out in public together when every instinct I had wanted to hold his hand or press a kiss to his check – claim him in the way that I was used to claiming someone I loved. We would never have that, he and I.

Now, the armor I'd subconsciously relied upon no longer had any weight or substance. There was no one to witness our affair. No way that we could get caught. We were stripped down to the studs, reduced to our most basic components without society there to hold us accountable for every perceived transgression. I was no different than any other woman he was interested in, and he had free rein to treat me as such. I didn't have to wonder if he wanted me; it was there in his kiss.

It's amazing really, how powerless words are when there is no one waiting to hear them. This was one of the reasons why I enjoyed sex. It made talking obsolete. Everything was simple and to the point, no room for games. Either someone was attracted to you or they weren't. That was something I understood, something I respected. A relief after spending months agonizing over every word, every smile, every text or lack thereof.

He wanted me. His kiss proved it. The fact that I was even here in the first place proved it. The terror that had arisen knowing that my walls no longer mattered softened. His hands on my body were better than any simple platitude or smiley emoji he could have given to me. Though, even with this new revelation, when the elevator started to slow, I panicked a little.

Pulling back from his embrace, I straightened my clothes. He chuckled and my face flamed. I was grown. The idea of being caught making out in the elevator by a stranger may not have been a big deal to anyone else, but for me it was instinct to pull away. To fear, deep down, that once those doors opened our secret would be on display for all the world to see.

It was a mark of just how special Zach made me feel that the fear passed almost as soon as it made itself known. He was amazing in that he could make me feel like a woman: sexy, wanted, interesting, regardless of the circumstances. It made me want to be more daring, more adventurous, and my shoulders straightened in defiance of my own reaction earlier.

'*I will enjoy this,*' I promised myself. No worrying, no second-guessing, no hesitating. I would throw myself fully into whatever the day might bring so that I could hold the memory of these hours with him close to my heart once I left. I would use them to help me get through the agonizing moments when I struggled to remember the sound of his voice or the precise shade of blue of his eyes.

Zach's apartment was a modernized one bedroom on the top floor of a twenty-one-story building. What should have been a painfully long elevator ride was over in what felt like seconds. Something about being kissed senselessly played havoc with my sense of time apparently. Not that I was complaining. The first thing I noticed when I stepped inside his apartment was the spectacular view of the Chicago skyline through his living room windows. Dark hardwood floors stretched throughout the space and the small kitchen off the living room was simply designed with its brown cabinets and stainless-steel refrigerator. There was a large, tacky red couch in the middle of the living area. Besides the couch, there was also a brown leather lazy boy and a giant bean bag chair stationed in a place of honor before his sixty-inch flat screen.

In short, it screamed bachelor pad and I instinctively thought of every episode I'd ever seen on HGTV as I mentally redecorated. Obviously, the couch would need to go, and it wouldn't hurt to have some art on the wall. Maybe a nice area rug in front of the television so that the kids could…

I stopped myself before the thought could carry me too far. My brain wanted to let the fantasy play out. What would it be like to see my kids here? Sitting comfortably in front of the television and rummaging through the refrigerator during the commercial breaks between cartoons.

There it was again. The urge to make plans for the future – as if it were ours to lay claim to. I had no business thinking about area rugs for his kids let alone how mine might get a kick out of his ugly ass couch if they ever got the chance to see it. I shook my head, clearing my mind of her, of the Brianna I'd promised myself to leave behind as soon as I'd stepped foot out of my house today. I couldn't have her with me here, not and take this step. The one that would drag me even further down the rabbit hole that was my relationship with Zach than ever before. She was a frightened thing, one in constant need of reassurance. Today wasn't about that, however. It wasn't about our relationship or where we did – and didn't – go from here. It was about enjoying one another and I needed the release of feeling wanted like it was a drug and I was struggling to stay clean.

"You want a drink?"

There it was. The anchor I needed was dressed in the smooth molasses rise and fall of his voice and the warmth of his hand against the small of my back. Zach led me towards his kitchen and I let him. I loved when he touched me. When he touched me, it was easy to forget the outside world. When he touched me, I stopped thinking so much and allowed myself to follow someone else's lead for once.

Sitting on one of the barstools at the kitchen counter, I watched as he made me a Tito's and tonic. There was music playing in the background that pulled the stress from my spine, weaving a spell around the two of us that made it seem as if being here together like this was the most natural thing in the world. We made idle chit chat, a part of me marveling at how clean and tidy his home was. Everything had a place and seemed meticulously maintained. I wondered if he was always this neat or if he'd cleaned up because he knew I was coming over. It was probably a bit of both. His office was just as organized and Zach was a man who prided himself on his control and I had the feeling that that extended to everything in his life. There were pictures of his kids hanging up here and there and the framed photos of their artwork was the only indication that this bachelor hadn't always been able to lay claim to the title.

Sipping my drink, I allowed the last of my hesitation and doubt to disappear. I gave myself permission to exist fully in the moment. Something I hadn't done since the first time we'd been intimate. Zach made his way around the counter and stood behind me, his hands on my shoulders and his breath a brand against the back of my neck. I shuddered, goosebumps rising all along my skin as he kneaded stiff muscles beneath an uncompromising grip. His strength always surprised me and even now I gasped as his thumbs worked a trail down my spine and back again. He was gentle, but there was a banked strength there that I couldn't deny.

This was what it must feel like to be on top of the world. To feel wanted and appreciated. I still couldn't believe that someone as handsome and successful as Zach could want someone like me. It baffled the mind. Though, had anyone asked I wouldn't have been able to explain exactly what I meant by 'someone like me.' At the time, it wasn't so much a turn of phrase as it was an overall sense of worthlessness. Some days with Zach only exacerbated that feeling. Leaving me convinced that he was going to wash his hands of me at any moment and that I'd never see him again. Those were the days when I clung to even the smallest act of kindness or affection from him.

I knew how it must make me look but couldn't help it, and my subsequent self-disgust was just icing on the cake. It was a vicious cycle; one I was still learning how to break free of. But that was only on some days. On others, being with Zach was like being a top model. Every move I made was poetry on display and he, a captive audience. On those days, I was a goddess. Aphrodite personified. On those days, my sexuality was both a weapon and gift wrapped in one.

On those days, I was unstoppable.

Today…today was one of those days.

Zach whispered something against the curve of my ear and pulled me to my feet. I giggled, turning into his arms as he increased the volume on the music and pulled me in tight and close. I wanted to kiss him again, to feel those hands traveling over my body again, but instead he nuzzled his face against my throat and lulled me into a dance. I wasn't a great dancer and for a moment awkwardness threatened to steal some of the brash confidence that anticipation had woven into my skin, but I wouldn't let it. Impressing him shouldn't have been so important to me still, but it was. I wanted to

be deserving of the attention he gave me, deserving of the way he

made me feel, and the only way that I knew how to do that was by

living up to and exceeding his expectations of me.

I forced myself to move in time with him and the music and

tried not to think too hard about what my arms were doing, or if I

was moving my hips to the beat, or if I had a dumb expression on my

face. So, we danced in the middle of his kitchen as he trailed

possessive fingers through my hair, across my breasts, and beyond. I

loved when he was playful with me, but I hated that he'd chosen now

to do it. I was so focused on not tripping over my own two feet that

thoughts I'd avoided by the skin of my teeth just minutes before

began whispering at me again.

I was skeptical, skeptical of what I was doing, and skeptical of

his intentions.

The awful part was that it was always there, that skepticism.

Impossible to escape or assuage unless I made a conscious,

concentrated effort to push it to the back of my mind. It was a relief

when he kissed me. It brought me back to the Brianna I wanted so

desperately to be for him. I slipped my tongue into his mouth,

shuddering with anticipation as he unbuttoned my jeans and worked

them down past my hips.

Was the music still playing? I wasn't sure. He bent me over the kitchen counter and the roaring in my ears drowned out everything else, including my own thoughts. The heat of him, the strength of him, it swallowed me whole. Left me gasping and squirming beneath him while he worked clever fingers within me. When I was ready, he pushed against my entrance until I welcomed him. We both cried out as he filled me and I became a mindless, hungry thing. All I wanted was for him to move. To finish what he'd started, what a part of me had been waiting for this entire time.

Then his hand was in my hair and he was wrapping the length of it around his fist so that he could use it like a leash, something to keep me in line and pull me close as his rhythm shifted and surged. It was funny, staring out the window at the sea of buildings that was Chicago, all I could think of was how lucky I was in that moment. He'd chosen *me* to have this kind of relationship with, to be intimate with. I saw a side to him that no one else was privy to; I was sure of it. And when he was inside of me this way, lost in the pleasure garnered by my body and my body alone, I was sure that what we had was real.

Somehow, we ended up in his bedroom. My shirt was gone and the blue comforter he laid me on was soft against the bare skin of my back. Much more comfortable than the unforgiving countertop had been against the weight of my breasts. Zach was still moving between my legs and I committed the sight of his face to my memory. The furrow between his brow, the intensity of his eyes, and the sweat that marred his skin. It was achingly familiar in that it was the same expression I'd seen on the face of every man I'd ever been with. A mixture of pleasure and intense concentration. Yet, for all its familiarity, it was something precious and worth remembering. Here was a snapshot of vulnerability. Something raw and basic. This was a version of Zach that no one else got to see and a surge of power and satisfaction filled me knowing that I was being given something in these moments that was reserved just for me.

I'm not sure how long we lay there, tangled in the sheets and breathing in one another, but by the time we finished my body was aching and exhausted. We were both sweaty but deeply satisfied. Curling up against him, I let my fingers trail across his chest and down his arms. Watching the fine hairs stand at attention with each delicate pass. His heart beat steadily beneath my ear and I sighed as he brushed my long hair aside to trace the length of my spine and the curve of my breast.

I wanted to stay in his arms forever, but I knew better.

Everything that I'd managed to push back was beginning to make its presence known once more and I found myself blurting out the very last thing I wanted to say to a man after hours of mind-blowing sex.

"Promise me something?"

"What?" he asked, voice gravelly with exhaustion.

"Promise me that you'll tell me if you start dating or having sex with someone else. It…it would hurt too much otherwise."

Just like that the air between the two of us chilled. I wanted to take the words back, but life didn't work that way, so instead I scrambled to say something, anything, that wouldn't make me sound clingy or needy.

"I just want a heads-up if you're getting serious with someone," I continued, and I couldn't help but feel as if I were digging myself a hole I wasn't equipped to climb back out of. I knew Zach was dating. He was newly divorced and had everything going for him. He was a man with options. I'd always accepted that. It wasn't the fact that he had options that scared me. It was the idea that he would explore those options while I was busy falling head over heels for him that broke me out in a cold sweat.

I wanted…no…

I *needed* him to be up front with me.

At the very least, if I knew what was going on, I could temper my emotions and perhaps save myself a world of heartbreak down the road. I would have loved to be as cavalier about our relationship as he was, but I couldn't afford to be that laid back when I wasn't even sure how to define the situation between the two of us. If anyone understood my concerns, it should have been Zach. He was the one who had been counseling me, the one who'd been helping me work through the mountain of doubts that seemed to plague me daily. But I didn't understand what I saw in that moment. For a second – just a second – his jaw went tight and his gaze guarded. It was over so quickly I may have imagined it and the softness of the smile that followed wiped the moment from my mind completely.

"Don't worry." Zach leaned in and kissed me on the forehead. "You have me all to yourself." He chuckled. "Unless I find someone as unique as you are. Then there might be some competition."

It must be magic, the way this man could unravel me with just a few simple words.

"Really?" I hated how hopeful I sounded, how moved. He may as well have said 'I love you.' I was so used to feeling dispensable that the idea that someone like Zach could find me unique and worthy of his attention took my breath away. It was only in those instances that I truly grasped just how demoralizing my childhood and all the years that followed had been for me. That even that small instance of acceptance was enough to leave me glowing.

What did he see in me? What was it about me that he found so special? The answer eluded me but I figured that if Zach could see something worth caring for in me then it must be there. If so, maybe I'd see it for myself one day.

The mood that afternoon changed between us after that. Zach didn't come out and say anything, but he didn't have to. It was like being at a party. At some point guests reached the silent agreement to disperse or go to bed. At some point, the fun simply stopped without so much as a warning. I rolled out of bed and squeezed myself back into my jeans. As I searched for my black wedges, Zach pulled on an old T-shirt, a worn pair of pants, and a visor. Looking at him like that, I wasn't thinking about how sexy he looked in casual clothes but about my grandmother of all people.

It was the visor. It was super nerdy and reminded me of my grandmother with her bright green visor and its spiral shoestring connecting in the back. She was infamous for wearing it anytime she was outdoors and the sun was anywhere in sight. Nerdy or not, I couldn't help but notice how cute he looked as he quietly sang along to the music playing from the speaker in the kitchen. We'd left the bedroom behind, and though I was exhausted his bedroom no longer felt as welcoming as it had. It was as if the very apartment were closing its doors to me, one by one, as the sun sunk further in the sky and the minutes flew by.

Soon I'd be back home and things would be business as usual. Though I didn't have to be back for a few more hours, I was already mentally preparing myself, already tucking the Brianna that Zach had caressed so lovingly only minutes before back in the box I kept her in. The box that protected me from her and vice versa. The box that was beginning to fray around the edges with every day that went by. I sat at the counter once more, perching on the edge of the barstool I'd already begun to think of as my own, and gathered my things. Zach made his way over to me and pressed his lips to mine.

It wasn't a romantic kiss, a welcoming kiss, a tantalizing kiss. Not like all the ones we'd shared before. If the kiss in the elevator had been 'hello,' then this one was 'goodbye.' Over and over again, gentle pecks that prompted me to laugh with forced amusement and place a hand against his chest.

"Are you rushing me out?" I lifted a brow just in case the sarcasm in my voice wasn't completely evident.

Despite my tone, I couldn't deny the flash of hurt when he smiled back and responded with suspicious quickness, "No. Of course not."

I didn't believe him but pushing the issue would do more harm than good. Soon after, my suspicions were all but confirmed when he made a show of checking the time and cursing beneath his breath.

"What's wrong?"

Shaking his head, Zach sighed and shot me a look filled with regret. "I'm such a dumbass, Bri. I completely forgot that I have something I'm supposed to do this afternoon."

My lips tightened until they felt practically bloodless. We'd been planning this day for weeks and he was only just remembering this *now*? Bullshit. But there was no way to prove it and the more I stewed over it the more disgusted I grew with myself. People made mistakes, even Zach. How many times had I double-booked myself? It didn't mean anything. I was probably just reaching because I was feeling insecure about going home. Zach cared for me. He'd said as much on more than one occasion. On top of that, he'd promised to tell me if he were seeing someone else. He wasn't trying to get rid of me so that he could sneak off to see someone else. He was better than that. *We* were better than that.

The reminder of our earlier conversation assuaged my suspicions, but only barely. When I left a few minutes later, I tried to pretend as if I did so because I was ready to leave anyway and not because he seemed anxious for me to go. Funny thing was, I don't think he believed my performance any more than I did his and I wondered if this is what love was and always would be: a badly written play where the actors were only barely convincing.

Where the audience clapped and 'oohed' and 'aahed' just to be polite and not because they found the events unfolding truly surprising. I tried to imagine being one of the audience members watching my life play out. What would I say about the actress sitting on that barstool, hands shaking as she checked her phone for messages from home?

Run?

This wasn't a slasher flick but still, it felt appropriate.

Watch out?

Maybe. I like to think that I would try and reserve judgment. At least until the last scene. But that brought about another question.

If I was waiting for the final curtain call, then which act was this?

Chapter Eleven

If I had to describe the overall theme of my life, it would have to be the small hand on a giant clock, ticking the seconds away. My relationship with Zach was on borrowed time and that fact was always at the front of my mind. Each encounter had a time restriction and Zach seemed all too willing to adhere to the restrictions placed on us. Given my situation, I was the last person who should have been allowed to complain but that didn't stop me from doing it anyway. Every moment with Zach was precious and it killed me that he didn't make more of an effort to spend as much time with me as possible.

I hated feeling as if I were nothing but an item to be checked off someone's to-do list. I didn't want to be scheduled, and I felt that if his intentions were real then he would make an effort to give me real time. Not the dregs of his day or a slot here and there when he had nothing else going on. If we met for lunch, it was always in between his clients. If I went to his job outside of my usual sessions, then there were either constant interruptions to contend with or I had to wait until he was able to pencil me into his otherwise full schedule.

The second time I was invited to his home ended much the same way as the first time had, with a forgotten plan heralding my unexpected departure. I understood that between work and his personal life, his time was always accounted for. I also understood that if I were as important to him as he claimed then he would have tried to make me more of a priority. If he wanted to be with me, he would have found the time. So, despite his constant reassurances of the opposite, I made peace with the fact that Zach didn't want any more from us than what we already had. He was all too happy to put in a minimal amount of effort.

That should have been warning enough on its own. After all, Chris had been doing the same for years. Even so, I wasn't ready to give up what little Zach was willing to give me. Even as half-assed as it was, the attention made me feel good and I was afraid to lose it. In hindsight, his affection grew to be a crutch. I couldn't find the love and acceptance I needed within myself so I searched for it in him. When he was gone, it was like a shadow had been cast across the sun and I was left cold and bereft. I could go from being on top of the world when he was there to struggling to keep my head above water whenever he ignored me for too long. The jump between joy and crippling depression was draining and I went through my days as skittish as a horse, constantly waiting for the next blow or for the other shoe to drop. Hyper-aware of every way that things could go wrong even when it was all going so, so right.

It left me frightened of going back to the reality that was my home life for too long where confusion of what was happening and what would happen plagued my every step. I needed something concrete to cling to, a port in the storm that was brewing. Zach should have been that port – I wanted him to be that port – and yet he wasn't. Despite this, I found myself reaching out to him more and more often for reassurance – which he was adept at providing by now. Briefly appeased, I would give him my all until the long stretches of not hearing from him once again drove me to reach out. Sometimes, I was afraid that I would waste away playing this game.

He should have a patent on it.

Oddly enough, Zach didn't seem to appreciate it when I accused him of playing games with me. During one of our conversations, he told me how sad it made him that I thought so negatively of myself.

"It's hard not to," I found myself saying. "I've been this way for so long that it's basically second nature."

Which was true. I was so used to thinking poorly of myself that it was my default. Somewhere along the line I had convinced myself that I didn't deserve happiness or love, so when I received these things there was always an undercurrent of disbelief. Of doubt.

Of fear.

"It doesn't have to be," he said, and I warmed. "I can show you that I care, if you'll let me."

At the time, it was impossible to tell what he meant. Did he actually care, or was he simply pretending to because of some need he had to 'fix' me? Fixing people was his job, after all. It wasn't far-fetched to believe that he was only going through the motions when it came to being with me. He was certainly capable of it; Zach knew what to say, how to say it, and when to get the response that he was looking for. In our early days together, I would have called him a people-pleaser.

Later? Manipulator.

You see, I wanted, desperately, to believe that Zach would be the exception to the rule. That he would be the one to prove that I deserved that picture-perfect kind of happiness that always seemed to come so easily to everyone else. But it was impossible to ignore the constant stream of excuses. I called him out on more than one occasion for toying with me, and he always knew exactly what to say to pull me right back in.

I didn't realize it at the time, but that conversation answered all my questions in just a few words. He was playing a part, and as long as he was willing to do so I was all too willing to play too. There came a day when his reassurances no longer assuage my fears, but by then I was too addicted to the attention I was getting from him. I was enamored by this parody of love and passion and I allowed it to cloud my common sense.

Something was off.

I could feel it.

All the signs were there.

The bizarre behavior and the lies disguised as explanations. More often than not, his actions didn't coincide with his words. Even so, I couldn't stop, couldn't pull myself away. I was an addict spiraling, knowing full well what I needed to do to bring this ride to a full stop but unable to bring myself to do it. My denial was only causing me pain, I could see that, but that still wasn't enough to get me to walk away.

I wanted to be happy.

Happiness was something that I had been searching for as long as I could remember and Zach gave that to me. When we were together, everything was perfect. So perfect that it made sense to ignore the not so perfect parts. Those moments of happiness were more precious than gold, mostly because of just how much the rest of my life had begun to spiral out of my control. I was no closer to figuring out what to do with my marriage and trying to maintain the balance between what I knew deep down was an emotionally abusive relationship with Zach and my relationship with Chris was overwhelming.

There were days when I couldn't leave the couch. Dishes were left at the table, the laundry baskets were overflowing, and general chaos reigned. It struck me more than once that if I wasn't the one maintaining our home, then it wouldn't be maintained and that only added to my growing sense of failure. My life was a game of Jenga and every new blow was another block gone missing until what was left barely stood.

Things would have been so much easier if I didn't feel the way that I did towards Zach and I wanted nothing more than to go back to those early days when he was nothing more than a therapist and friend. Why was I doing this to myself? Why was I torturing myself this way? I had no answers and with every month that passed, the problem only grew.

Chris could sense that my attention was somewhere else. He would have had to be blind not to notice that there was *something* going on with me. I was reticent and withdrawn. With the state of the house often falling into disrepair, it would have been impossible not to pick up on my frequent bouts of melancholy. He continued to make an effort, but I was no longer interested in spending any time with him. There was a disconnect between us, a chasm that grew wider with every failed interaction and snippy tone.

When Zach and I were apart for long periods of time, I would test the waters at home. I was trying to see if there was anything there worth saving. If distance from Zach would give me the perspective I needed to see my husband again. To love him again, like I used to. While I still loved him, I grew to realize that it wasn't at all the same anymore. I found him boring, uninteresting. It wasn't just because of Zach either. Chris and I had been growing apart for years. There was something about him that was content with remaining stagnant. There always had been. While I was busy trying to find myself, Chris was content to get lost in the routine of life. He was always willing to settle, always willing to stagnate whereas I hungered for something more.

I changed.

He didn't.

And inevitably, I had to accept the fact that we had grown apart and I couldn't even pinpoint the exact moment when it had happened.

The arguments between Chris and me continued and grew in frequency if not volume. We were in unspoken agreement to try and not to tear into one another in front of the boys. We didn't always succeed, but at least we tried. In many ways it reminded me painfully of my own childhood and to compensate for that, I struggled to hide how I was feeling from them as much as possible. At eight, five, and four my children meant the world to me and it killed me to think that I was failing them in any way. Despite my best intentions, it was a struggle to try and be a good mom while my mind and emotions were in an upheaval.

My turmoil seemed contagious and I didn't want to pass it on to my kids. Already it was wearing away at what remained of my relationship with Chris and eroding my friendships. I still felt as isolated as ever. While Tiffany was also having an affair, she seemed to be having fun and it was awkward to complain to her about what I was going through when there was nothing concrete that I could point to as being the problem.

So what if he didn't spend as much time with me as I wanted?

So what if weeks at a time sometimes went by without a word?

When I said them aloud, they didn't sound as bad. They certainly didn't sound serious enough to account for how tortured I felt. But that was what made emotional abuse so dangerous. On the surface, it looked innocent enough. No one else could see just how deeply some things could cut. What hurt me could seem inconsequential to Tiffany, and I was hesitant to share. Especially with someone so wrapped up in their own situation. It wasn't that she was self-centered, so much as she was sometimes so focused on her own life that no one else even made it onto her radar.

Over the next six months, it grew harder for me to cope with things. When the burden grew too heavy, I found another therapist. A woman, this time. Her name was Anne and she was understandably alarmed by my relationship with Zach. She helped me see just how much of his behavior was designed to manipulate me, though I was still in a fair amount of denial. The first time I went to her office, I was embarrassed because Anne was someone I had been seeing before. I stopped going to her for a few years before deciding to start our session once again to discuss Zach. Opening up to her was hard at first, but I was so desperate for help that I eventually found the words I needed to tell my story.

"None of this is your fault, Bri," she told me sternly. By then I had already seen her several times and this was a point she made often. "What Zachary is doing is completely unprofessional and goes against every code we have."

It scared me when she talked like that because the last thing I wanted was for Zach to get into trouble because of us. My first instinct was always to defend him, to remind her that I was a grown woman and a willing participant, but I knew where that road ended.

Willing or not, grown woman or not, it's still an abuse of power. He took advantage of your vulnerability to encourage a physical relationship when he should have been helping you figure out why you felt the way that you did towards him.'

I could never find the words to counter that with, and it was easier just to avoid that line of conversation. Anne claimed more than once that there was something off about Zach.

"He's not all there."

"What do you mean?"

Anne shook her head thoughtfully. "From what you've told me he seems to have an issue with making any real emotional connections. He dabbles at them, goes through the motions, but I doubt that it's anything more than that. To string along a patient, especially one with your history, is dangerously irresponsible. I wouldn't be surprised if he's done this before."

Zach wasn't the only one we talked about either.

"I'm sorry, Bri, I just don't think there's anything there to mend." The way she shook her head and the look in her eyes showed real regret. Chris was another hotly contested topic of conversation. Anne didn't believe that we would last, but I couldn't afford to think that way. How could I be sure that there was nothing there to save when Zach had my emotions tied up in knots? I couldn't afford to throw my marriage away without being sure that I was doing the right thing. Would Chris and I have drifted so far apart if Zach and I had never been together? Would I be struggling with the same sense of restlessness, the need for change, if I wasn't cheating?

I didn't know.

Because I didn't know, I was unwilling to make such a huge life decision just yet. If it were just me? Maybe. But there were the kids to think about as well. Sometimes I wondered what was worse? Sticking it out in an unhappy marriage or tearing our family apart and starting from a clean slate? Which would scar them the least? *Was* there an option that didn't guarantee that my kids would one day find themselves sitting across from a psychiatrist? There was so much to consider, and while Anne didn't have all the answers for me, talking to her did offer a modicum of relief. She was calm, kind, and sympathetic and I needed that. It was the validation I needed that my infidelity hadn't made me an awful person.

The pills Anne had for me were hard to swallow, but that was the reason I liked her. She didn't hold back any punches, but neither did she judge, and seeing her twice a month helped keep me sane. When all I wanted was to curl up into a ball and disappear, her no-nonsense acceptance was a much-needed change of pace. I began seeing her six months into the relationship with Zach, however, and by then I was in so deep that it would have taken more than a few conversations to pull me back out.

I needed him. I needed him to distract me from my life, from the dismal gray that filled my thoughts when I was alone and the air lay quiet. Though I knew better, Zach still brought me joy in those brief moments we spent together. While some of our encounters over the next few months were intimate, the sex eventually stopped. I craved more from him in those moments, but one day the heat was simply…gone. It worried me at first, but each time we saw one another I was comforted by the fact that Zach was still around. It was proof that he was spending time with me because he really felt something for me. It wasn't just physical, which is something I feared may have been the case.

Why else would he waste his time maintaining a relationship with me? I'd grown used to the idea of the physical being the be-all and end-all of what it meant to be fulfilled in a romantic relationship. With sex off the table, there was nothing for him to gain from being with me, so the fact that he stuck around must mean something. That's what I told myself anyway. Anything to keep pretending that the two of us were OK.

That we would last.

I was always wondering when I would hear from Zach next and reaching out to him had become instinctive. It didn't matter that he was the cause of my discontent. I needed the sound of his voice, or the sight of his dry humor over text messages to get me through another day without being able to touch or see him. I often poured my heart to him, begging him to please tell me when all of this was over and not to simply disappear on me. The terror of being hurt by him was crippling in its intensity, just as he knew it would be. Zach was the one person who knew how truly fragile I was. Who knew just how much I needed a gentle hand. For most of my life it had been impossible for me to let things go because I was never able to get any closure for what truly mattered.

Zach had become something that mattered, and I needed to know when things would be coming to an end between us so that I could learn how to let him go. I trusted that he knew that. That he would do right by me when we finally reached our inevitable conclusion.

Zach was someone whom I had put all my trust into. He wouldn't hurt me. He couldn't. Whenever my emotions boiled over, he was there, apologizing for being gone for so long, telling me how much he cared for me, assuring me that he would always be there no matter the nature of our relationship.

"We're still friends. I'm still going to be there for you, even if we aren't sleeping together. How about we have lunch next week? My 1:00 pm appointment canceled so I have a little extra time to kill."

And round and round we went.

I gave him every opportunity to tell me when it was over. To let me down the way that I needed. Instead he fed me hope. Hope that there could be more for us if only I had a little faith. I wanted to believe him.

So, I did.

Chapter Twelve

Zach and I would have a lot of conversations about how things between us would never work. Which means that the end shouldn't have felt like a punch to the gut, only it did. Things came about simply enough. Zach told me that he was going on a trip to the Philippines with his family.

"That sounds fun." I was jealous. A vacation would have been nice right about then, and on top of that going on a trip with Zach would have felt like a dream. Yet one more thing that the two of us would never have, I supposed.

He laughed. "Not really, but everyone is looking forward to it. I'd much rather stay home in bed." The tone in his voice implied that he would've liked having me by his side for that. This was before the two of us had stopped having sex altogether, but our intimacy level had definitely dropped significantly by that point. We flirted for a few more minutes, the reminder of the tenderness we shared a welcome break from the otherwise monotony of my day. I wished him a safe trip with my pulse fluttering and the memory of his arms around me still fresh in my mind. I remember distinctly when he got back into town from his trip because he called me late that night and asked if there was any way that the two of us could meet up.

"Sorry for calling so late." He sounded relaxed and in high spirits. The Philippines must have been fun. "I'm jet-lagged as hell." A pause. Then, "Where are you right now? Can I see you?"

Zach had this magical power to make a booty call seem like anything but. I never fell for it, but I still played along because that's what the two of us did. It was our dynamic and in a weird way, it worked for us. I was never exactly sure why. Maybe it's what happened when two lost people searched for belonging with one another. On the surface, it seemed like Zach had everything under control. That he could do no wrong. I'll admit that for a little while, I'd fallen for it. It wasn't until I really got to know him that I understood that it was just a mask. Much like the one I often wore these days. As the passion between Zach and me cooled, things at home grew harder to ignore. With Zach going MIA more often, I needed a support system more than ever before.

Tiffany and I were close, but as time progressed, I began to feel more and more like nothing but a sounding board. After she started her affair it was like her personality did a complete 180. Tiffany had given birth to her third child a few years before the affair, before she and her family moved into a larger house. After the move, they needed the extra income. So, with their two older children in school all day and a nanny to watch their youngest, Tiffany returned to work as soon as she had the opportunity to do so. It was there that she and a coworker began to hit it off. The two worked together more often than not and many of their company events lasted long into the night. Business lunches and overnight trips with just the two of them was a chance for her to indulge. Especially when it came to the more social aspect of her job. Their ability to see clients early in the day allowed them the opportunity to use the rest of their time to drink before work was over.

And they partook.

Often.

In fact, Tiffany would come by my house two to three times a week just so she could sober up before making her way home. While we talked about my issues and she tried to be supportive, her situation definitely took precedence over what I had going on. Which didn't help ease the weight that I was under. I so desperately wanted to feel unburdened, but I couldn't with her. Not because we weren't close enough; I considered Tiffany a sister and I looked up to her. Though I couldn't understand how she was able to cheat without acting any differently with her husband. Taking another man to bed didn't seem to affect her at all and her actions often left me confused.

It was like she was acting out this fantasy life where there were no real-world problems or consequences. A part of me envied her while another part continued to worry about her and her behavior. Despite everything, or maybe because of it all, Tiffany and I continued to grow closer as friends. I knew that there was something off about what was going on with her, but I just wanted her to be alright.

One person that I could count on throughout the entire affair, besides Anne and Tiffany, was my brother, Michael. I'd always been close with my family and he was the one person I could share almost anything with. I needed the support of someone who knew Zach, Chris, and me and who wouldn't let the truth slip. It also helped to have a sympathetic ear who was willing to let me vent without trying to either analyze me or use me for something.

Michael and I were eighteen months apart and were as thick as thieves. Which was no surprise really; we'd been a part of one another's lives for over twenty years. Tall and scrawny with dark eyes and an enviably free spirit, he was as opinionated as he was caring. It was devastating when, shortly after graduating high school, we cut ties with one another after a family feud put the two of us at odds.

For almost three years we didn't speak at all only to reconnect at my stepsister's wedding. We'd been working on rebuilding our relationship back to where it had been ever since. Which was why, when he told me that there was something he felt I needed to know about Zach, I listened.

"So, it turns out your boy toy is in a relationship."

I froze, my mind going blank. "First of all, stop calling him that." I knew he was only teasing so my reprimand lacked any heat. "Second of all, what are you talking about? What relationship?"

"It's on Facebook," he continued. "Apparently he's dating some woman named Jenifer. I've been cyber stalking her for like, twenty minutes and it seems pretty serious."

I was stunned. It was true that things had been more distant than usual between us lately. Something I'd noted the last time I'd been at his apartment. Things had been a lot different than the first time I'd visited. For one, we weren't intimate. In fact, when I think back on it Zach sat as far away from me as he could. The conversation started off casually, but soon shifted.

"I'm hurting." I hated the way my voice cracked, and I hated how unsure and frightened I sounded, but there was no helping it. "It feels like all I do is cry these days."

"Bri—"

"Don't." I shook my head before he could finish. I hated when he took that tone with me, as if this was just another session and that I was somehow overreacting. I could feel the difference between us and I knew that there was something wrong, I just couldn't put my finger on what and Zach was no help.

"I know you're confused," he told me, his eyes intent on mine. "But you don't have to be. Bri, I care about you. You have to know that by now."

We spoke for a while longer and I pushed my anxiety down long enough to fake a smile or two. Zach's passion for me was cooling – that much had become clear over the last several weeks. That didn't stop him from flirting and making comments about my butt as he walked me out of his apartment and to the elevator. The disconnect was agonizing. Why would he act as if he wanted me and then refuse to touch me? Maybe I just wasn't good enough. Maybe he would still be interested now if I'd been able to relax all the times we'd been together. I was so tired of overthinking our situation, but I couldn't seem to help myself despite my best efforts. There were times when I told myself that I would be happy with whatever I could get so long as Zach still wanted to be a part of my life, to see me. I still thought that what we had was special even though sex wasn't the only thing missing these days when it came to Zach and me. He was texting me less and less and seemed not to care one way or another about seeing me. I told myself that he just had a lot going on in his personal life, that I was being overly sensitive, but my justifications rang false.

Too afraid of coming across as needy, I refrained from calling him out on anything. I was sure that I'd just drive him away. I ended up fighting the urge to contact him until the need to speak to him became too much to handle and I crumbled. Over the course of several weeks I would get odd texts late at night. Texts I wasn't sure how to respond to and wasn't sure if I would want to if I did. I would hear from him the next morning and it was always something along the lines of 'I thought I might see you last night.'

It was just one of the many ways that he continued to make me feel as if he wanted me. His constant reassurances of how much I meant to him were beginning to do more harm than good. I hadn't been exaggerating when I told him that it felt like all I did lately was cry. I spent most of my days in tears wondering why I couldn't seem to put an end to all of this. I'd even gone so far as to research patient/therapist relationships to understand why I was so emotionally attached and to prove – if only to myself – that what I felt was different.

Real.

Instead, I came across the idea of Transference.

Basically, it was when a patient took emotions they should – or did – feel towards someone else (usually a parent) and redirected those feelings onto the psychiatrist. I couldn't help but see the correlation, but I refused to accept it. We *were* different. For one thing, we had a past. He had been a part of my life for so long and he wouldn't leave when the sex ended, and that's all I needed to keep going.

Like the tides, my moods rose high and sunk low in a never-ending dance. Weeks passed and I found myself pouring my heart out to him yet again. He suggested that we get together and explained all of the reasons why we couldn't be together.

As if I didn't already know.

As if *I* hadn't expressed most of these points during the course of our relationship.

"We'll always be friends, Bri."

I felt as if I were going to be sick.

"I'll never stop being a support system for you," he continued. "I care too much about you to ever disappear on you like that."

Even then, in that jarring exchange, I knew that there was something else going on. Something he wasn't telling me. His voice was warm, kind, but there was a distance that reminded me of our sessions together. *'He's seeing someone,'* I thought, musing like smoke. Coming from nowhere in particular and staining the air around it. *'He just doesn't want to tell me.'* It would certainly explain how he could go from hot to cold so quickly. Something was causing his distance and yet when I broached the subject, he was quick to promise that nothing like that was going on.

I shook my head, still doubtful.

"Look me in the eye and tell me you aren't dating anyone."

He met my eyes, his gaze just as unflinching as always.

"Brianna, I swear. I'm not seeing anyone. There's only you."

That was two days ago.

Now Michael was telling me something completely different. I was used to dismissing any naysayers when it came to Zach and me, but not Michael. Coming from Michael, the warning hit closer to home and I got on Facebook immediately to see for myself. A pit was growing in my stomach and my heart sinking was a physical pain that left me short of breath. He'd lied to me. I'd trusted him, and he'd lied to me.

I reached out immediately, too distraught to stop myself from acting on instinct. It was a shock to the system when he not only apologized but promised to see me right away. I was sure that he would have tried to deny it or, at the very least, dismiss me as if my outrage didn't matter. The fact that he took my feelings seriously and even went so far as to invite me over to talk things through blindsided me. He was still working at the school when he wasn't taking clients at his office, and by the time I shook myself out of my daze I was sitting in the same spot I'd used to sit as a teenager. As he'd done so often before, he sat across from me as we spoke and I couldn't help but notice how less personable our interaction was.

"Do you have any idea how devastated I am?" I struggled to hold back tears, but in the end it was a losing battle. "How could you lie to me? I *trusted* you." I was shaking, trying to keep my voice level when all I wanted to do was yell at him. It felt as if there were hooks in my windpipe, pulling me apart and making it hard to breathe but I knew that was only a barely contained crying jag threatening to overtake the last of my senses. "If you were just going to play with my emotions—"

"I'm not playing with anything, Brianna," he interrupted. "I care about you. I could never lie about something like that." Hearing him call me 'Brianna' instead of 'Bri' was yet another betrayal, yet another league in the space stretching out between us. How could he not see it? Or could he see it just fine and he was lying to me even now?

"Really?" I snapped. "Then what about your girlfriend?" My words tasted bitter on my tongue. There was no denying my jealousy. This woman was able to have all of him and envy was a band around my heart that he had never bothered to try and give me more. "If you cared about me at all, I wouldn't have had to find out this way. Through *Facebook*. Do you have any idea what it did to me when I realized I would have to mourn the loss of you? How devastated I was?"

To my chagrin, he chuckled and I couldn't help but feel like an angsty teenager coming to lament about my life. It was a feeling I didn't appreciate though his next words dispelled my annoyance.

"So what if I'm dating someone?" he asked. "That doesn't mean we can't still see each other. I could never not be there for you, Bri."

In just three sentences, I was right back to square one. What the hell did he mean? Where did that put me in his life, where did it put us in mine? It would have been kinder if he'd just made a clean break of things then and there, but no. Instead he gifted me with fodder to dwell on for the next several days. I made the mistake of asking him how long they'd been dating. Looking back through our correspondences for matching dates and times I realized that during the time when he was seeing her, he was still actively reaching out to me and trying to get me to come over. In fact, I learned that he'd gone to the Philippines and not his family the way he'd claimed.

Realizing just how much he'd been lying to me left me sick to the stomach. What else had he been dishonest about? How long had he been stringing me along? Had anything been real or was it all just a game to him – a way to pass the time? Despite all the red flags, I still believed him when he told me that he cared. That what we had was special – even though he was emotionally invested in someone else.

Maybe I needed to believe those things because the alternative would have broken me. I've never been so open and honest with anyone in my life, never been so up front and in tune with my own feelings. Zach was there to lean on when I needed him but he was also the one who pulled me out of my darkest places when I couldn't. When I felt ugly or not good enough, he gave me confidence. Most importantly, he made me want to *be* confident. To have that trust betrayed left me reeling and unsure.

It took a few days, but the shock and sadness faded and I was able to make peace with the situation. Yes, Zach was kind of a jerk but he held such a special place in my life that I couldn't let him go. This was actually a good thing. Now that he was dating someone, I could take some time and focus on my own life and the two of us could maintain our special bond. It was a situation that I could live with. Miraculously, knowing that he was with someone allowed me to settle into a headspace where I wasn't anxious in between calls and texts anymore. I even learned to expect his absences, excuses, and delayed responses. He was still a part of my life and that's all that mattered.

With things with Zach finally resolved, it was easier to shift my focus to my feelings for Chris. I was no longer waiting for anything from Zach. That situation was going to be whatever it was going to be, but there were still unanswered questions when it came to my marriage.

I wanted things at home to be easier now that I wasn't as distracted, but it was the exact opposite. It hurt because now that I was able to separate Chris and Zach emotionally, I should have been able to reconnect with my husband. Only, I couldn't. The days that followed were the darkest they've ever been. For the first time since I was a teenager, I found myself questioning my life. Things that used to matter left me feeling empty now and I couldn't find joy or purpose in what remained, including my relationship with Chris.

What have I been doing with my life? I was nowhere near where I thought I should be in terms of success or love, and once I started cataloging my own perceived failures, I sunk even lower than I ever would have thought possible. The only thing keeping me afloat were my kids. I struggled to hold it together for them, but behind every fake smile was the urge to reach out to Zach. I needed him now more than ever to tell me that everything was OK, to give me some advice or an encouraging word or two. Nearly a month had passed since I'd last seen him and when he shot me a text saying that we would talk over the weekend and set up a time for us to see one another, it was like a light at the end of a very long tunnel.

There he was again, coming through for me when I needed him the most. I was so grateful for that, for him and the fact that he was still taking time out of his life for me and I didn't hesitate to tell him as much. That Monday, he texted me again saying that he would contact me later on that afternoon. Since I knew that we wouldn't get much time to talk, I rehearsed what I wanted to say over and over again as I waited by the phone that day. Hours passed but I wasn't surprised or hurt when I looked up and realized that the sun was already sinking in the sky and I still hadn't heard from him. By now, this was our new normal and I was sure that I would be hearing some excuse later tonight or the next day about what happened. Then we would reschedule and talk some other time.

It was 6:18 pm when my phone finally went off.

"Bri…I believe you are way stronger than you think you are. I've always thought that. Looking back at our communication, it's very clear to me that I should have listened to you all along when you told me to be clear with my intentions. I made choices to be vague, thinking that would help you to see that I care about you...instead all it did was confuse you and make things more painful for you. I know that you will move on from this. I need to be very clear. I am not the healthy or the right person for you to be seeking for support. Please lean on your family and friends for support. They can truly help you more than I can. I want to make this easier for you. I know it will be painful at first, but I want to make the healthy choice and to disconnect any temptation you may have to contact me. Therefore, I will be blocking all communication. I wish you all the love and self-care you deserve."

Chapter Thirteen

It was April 30, 2018, in the late afternoon when my world shattered. I remember it like it was yesterday. What had just happened? How could he just delete my entire existence that way? Why would he pretend as if he loved me only to throw me away in the end? Through *text messages* of all things. He didn't even have the decency to break my heart to my face and yet he could look me in the eye and lie about a whole ass girlfriend?

I didn't understand, and the questions spiraled through my mind like a wildfire, burning everything they touched. We had plans to talk, to see each other. Why was this happening all of a sudden? It was crushing, the weight of the emotion struggling for dominance within me. I couldn't decide which was stronger: the rage, the hurt, the sadness, or the gut-wrenching fear.

Fear.

That's what it all boiled down to. An unrelenting fear. Fear of losing Zach. Fear of what that loss meant? Fear of being alone with this growing darkness within me and my one lifeline snatched away. I called Michael on my way to a nearby bar, the tears so thick and heavy that I could barely get the words out to explain what had happened. He was irate and so was my sister when she met up with me a few minutes later for drinks. We spent the next couple of hours trying to piece everything together. All I was doing was torturing myself. I knew that. Yet it was all I could do now that Zach refused to speak to me.

The only measure of control I had left.

Two drinks later and I was still no closer to the closure I so desperately craved. I left the bar only to sit in my car. I broke down again before I was even fully settled behind the wheel. The thought of going home at that moment left me physically ill. All I could think of was how there was no faking this. I couldn't face my kids or Chris and pretend as if I was OK. *Nothing* was OK and I didn't think it ever would be again. I was a mess – not just physically and mentally tapped out but grieving in a way that went down to my very bones. There was no way I could put on a brave face, not this time. Desperate for an alternative, something to stall the inevitable, I decided to call my parents.

When I showed up that night, crying hysterically as I confessed the entire sordid mess, 'shocked' would have been too mild a word for the expression on their faces. Thankfully they seemed more interested in soothing me than judging me and I cried until there was nothing left in me to give. It felt as if I'd been run over by a bus, but somehow I managed to drive myself home where I proceeded to drink.

I drank until the pain became a dull, throbbing noise. Until the memory of the last several hours grew blurry and indistinct. Until the world went dark and I vaguely found myself wondering if this was what my own mother used to go through, that helpless moment when the bottle seemed the only recourse – a savior and a punishment all rolled into one.

When I woke up, it was 4:00 am. The numbers were judgmental sentinels on my phone screen, the light from the display so bright that it dug its way into my brain via my retinas and set up shop with a hammer and anvil.

An unrelenting beat.

My eyes were so swollen from crying that it was difficult to see and just when I thought there was nothing left, the tears came again. My breath caught in my chest, and for a terrifying moment I forgot what it was to breathe. I tried to stem the flow, biting my lip and burying my face in my pillow to muffle the hollow, broken sounds I made so I wouldn't wake anyone. I sounded like a wounded animal.

I *felt* like a wounded animal.

Like someone had carved a chunk out of me and left me bleeding and broken. What hurt even more was that there was no one to turn to. Confessing to my family had gotten me through the initial onslaught but it had done nothing to stem the tide. I was drowning, sinking, and all the darkness that had already been in the stands – waiting – reared up above me and came crashing down to swallow me whole. I lost my footing, stumbled, and panic surged and took all rational thought.

I curled in on myself, aching, all clenched teeth and animal-like desperation. If I could have escaped my own body in that moment, if I could have gnawed through a limb and found freedom, I would have fled the pain. But no. I was trapped, even more so now than I'd ever been in my marriage with Chris. How long I lay there, wrapped in my own misery and unable to quell it, I don't know. Eventually my eyes grew too tired and swollen to stay open and the panic attack eased enough to allow my body to collapse into sleep. Not the unconsciousness that came from too much alcohol, but some parody of rest.

My alarm went off at 6:30 the next morning and I could have cried again for how painfully normal and familiar it all was. Why was the world still going about its business as if the bombshell that had just been dropped on me didn't matter? It was the same thing I found myself wondering after Natalie died. She must have been going through so much pain and yet the sun still rose and set as if none of it had ever been worth a damn. Realistically, I knew that my problems didn't matter in the grand scheme of things, but that didn't help me feel any better. Instead it just left me feeling even more alone in my misery, insignificant in this grief that should have been earth-shattering.

With the sun rising, there was no time to dwell on my pain. After all, there were lunches to make and kids to take to school. A mask to maintain. I knew what I had to do, but I dreaded getting out of bed. My body felt paralyzed. My limbs too heavy to move. There was a weight on my chest that made it hard to draw in a full breath and I shuddered wondering if this was all the precursor to another panic attack.

Somehow, I managed to get out of bed. Sluggishly, I made lunch for my sons and loaded the kids into the car. I was proud of myself for holding it together. In fact, I may have even managed a smile as I waved goodbye. Moving was good, I decided. As long as I was moving, as long as I was doing something, then I didn't have to think. Any time that I had to think, to be still, was an opportunity for the tears to resurface. I almost broke down at a red light, but the radio offered a much-needed distraction until I managed to stumble back into the house. Once inside, I allowed myself to break down again.

My own reaction frightened me. I couldn't control it, I couldn't find my way out of it. Grabbing for my phone, I called Anne and made a last-minute appointment. When she agreed to see me at 1:00 pm, gratitude left me shaking. I wasn't sure I could make it through the day without someone there to help me work through the mess I'd found myself in. As soon as she saw me, she seemed to know that I was teetering on a very high ledge. Talking to her helped level me out, just enough for me to promise her and myself that I would try and pull it together. I couldn't allow this pain to bring me down. I *had* to be stronger than it was or it really would break me.

'Yeah, easier said than done,' I thought hours later, staring at the bottle of vodka on my kitchen counter, unsure whether it was an enemy or an ally. *'It's a nice plan. In theory, anyway.'* The reality proved much harsher. Harder to handle. For what was probably the first time in my life I understood what my mother must have been going through in the years before she died. I knew that she was battling

with something, something bigger than she could handle on her own. The alcohol didn't erase my pain, but it helped me forget for a little while, helped numb the realization that no one understood what I was feeling or what I was going through.

Two years.

I'd dedicated two years of my life to my relationship with Zach and he'd thrown it all away as if none of it had ever meant a thing. The moments we'd spent together blurred in my mind, and I found myself going over every meeting and conversation, every kiss, every promise until the pain compounded into something bigger than just a shot or two could handle. The next several days went by in a haze. I couldn't seem to pull myself together enough to get things done around the house and I struggled to brush my hair and put on makeup each morning. Worst of all, I kept breaking down in front of my kids. It broke me to see their looks of concern when they saw me crying. I tried to explain that mommy was just a little sad, but that didn't ease their concern.

Since I babysat on Wednesdays, I tried to function somewhat normally. The best I could manage was hiding in the bathroom, coming out only to make lunches and snacks. Too drained to interact the way I usually did, I sat everyone in front of the television while I grieved. As soon as they left, I turned to the bottle of vodka again, drinking until I was finally able to drag myself to bed.

Thursday morning came and the pain was no easier to bear than it had been the last few days. Unable to stop myself, I reached out through his work email. It hadn't taken me long to realize that he'd blocked me everywhere else and it was the only way I could think of to reach him. I knew it would be better if I just followed his lead and broke off all contact cold turkey, but I couldn't. I needed answers. Something, anything to give me closure. He owed me that much. After dropping my two oldest boys off at school, I headed to the store with my youngest in tow. A little retail therapy would do me good. It might have even made me feel better if I hadn't checked my phone before we stepped inside and saw his name in my inbox.

"I don't want to be the source of your pain anymore, do not contact me on here. I will not be contacting you. You need to try to get over this."

I wanted to scream. Instead I swallowed the words that wanted to spill forth and tried not to lose control of myself. How was I supposed to react in this situation? Was I meant to rant and rave? Drive up to his job and call him out for all his lies? The possibilities ran through my head, different scenarios playing out in high definition, but nothing felt right. In all honesty, I felt empty and that emptiness seemed to be growing larger by the second. I was desperate to stop the spread of it, but I knew the only thing that could was Zach. I *needed* him to hear me. To fully grasp what he'd done and acknowledge how much it had hurt me. The idea that he could just toss me aside and cut off all contact with me as if I didn't deserve even an explanation was intolerable. My thoughts were so crowded and disjointed I couldn't even shop. My son and I left the store after only a few minutes and I hadn't even pulled out of the parking lot before I was crying again.

Pretty soon I would need to pick my son up from preschool and I would need to pull myself together by then. Hoping for a distraction and a sympathetic ear, I made my way over to my sister's house. I showed up on her doorstep unannounced, my aviators doing a poor job of hiding a fresh wave of tears. I stayed until it was time to pick my son up from school and drop my youngest off. Throughout the day I kept asking myself the same question over and over again.

How?

How could he do this to me?

After walking into the school, I returned to my car and checked my phone while my son chattered in the background about his day. I'd never bothered looking into Zach, but now that he'd cut off communication that was the first thing I thought to do. I entered his name into the search engine and my breath caught as review after review popped up.

'...*sexual predator*'

'*intimacy addict...*'

The type burned like a brand into my mind and my pulse raced. No. No, no, no. This wasn't possible. He'd always been so kind. Had always made me feel so special. There was no way the man I knew and the one mentioned in these reviews were the same person.

Except...

Something about the accusations struck a chord within me. The simple fact that someone had gone through the trouble to write these reviews meant that I wasn't the first woman he'd crossed a line with. Exactly how many times had he done this? Who else had he made feel special? Who else had he made false promises to? Lied to? Something about knowing that there were other women out there who had gone through the same thing that I was turned the sadness into anger.

I caught sight of myself in my rearview mirror as I drove and it struck me that I didn't recognize the woman I'd become. I'd always seen myself as an honest and kindhearted person. Someone who was loyal to a fault. Yet, since reconnecting with Zach I hadn't been – not to myself, not to my husband, my family, or my friends. I'd chosen the path of active ignorance, so desperate for kindness and the affection that I wasn't getting at home to look beneath the surface. I'd never learned how to love myself and that had left me vulnerable and easy to manipulate. In the end I'd fallen right into the palm of his hand even though I knew deep down that something was wrong.

Over the next few weeks, I found it nearly impossible to reconcile the Zach I knew with the man portrayed in the reviews I'd read. I knew that a part of my denial was thanks to this inherent need I had to protect him, even now. I went so far as to call everyone in my family and accuse them of writing the reviews in a misguided bid to protect me. But there was no way that they could have, or would have, done anything like that. Something wasn't adding up. The man in those reviews wasn't Zach. It couldn't be. And yet I didn't know how someone could post all those things if there wasn't a story there.

Emotionally, I was a wreck. Knowing that there was no way I could continue as I was and hoping for some answers, I reached out to his boss, Jackie. If it turned out that my lingering faith in him was misplaced and I was a victim, I would need proof that he'd been my therapist in the first place so I asked her if there was any record of me being one of Zach's patients. I wanted to get a feel for what was going on without revealing too much, but she told me that his patient information was something that she didn't have access to.

"I can get in touch with him for you if you—"

"No," I interrupted, a flash of panic like a knife to my middle. If she mentioned my name to him…what if he thought I was the one who'd written those reviews to hurt him? As far as Zach knew, I was looking for ways to get him into trouble. "Thank you, but no." This time I sounded much calmer. "If I need to get in touch with him, I can. I just wanted to check with you first."

We spoke for a few minutes more and just as I was getting ready to hang up, another question occurred to me.

"By the way, does Dr. Harris still work there?" I tried to sound as casual as possible but I'm sure some of my nerves leaked through. If Zach had been fired then that was proof that there was something serious going on. Which meant that there might be some credibility to those reviews after all.

"Of course." She hesitated. "Unfortunately, Dr. Harris won't be available for a while due to some personal issues."

If anything, the conversation left me with more questions than I'd started off with. It also left me with the uncomfortable realization that I still cared for Zach, even if he had been using me. It made me even more determined to get to the bottom of everything. Luckily, my dad offered to do some investigating of his own. Zach was nowhere to be found in the Illinois Department of Financial and

Professional Regulation database. Which made no sense as he would have to be licensed as a social worker for the school. Digging a little deeper, I pulled up any information that I could about Jackie. I was able to tell from that search that her license was active, so at least I knew I was doing it correctly.

Maybe the reason I couldn't pull up anything on Zach was because he was being investigated by the state. There was no way of knowing for sure and my fear that there was some truth to be found in those reviews after all grew. Days passed and it was hard to tell which emotion was stronger: the disgust at the thought that he could be capable of doing something like this, the shame of knowing that I'd been a naïve participant in his charade, or the anger. Anger at him, yes, but mostly at myself for putting myself in a situation where he could use me the way that he had.

It lit a fire under me and I spent every free moment that I had trying to figure out exactly what was going on. I called the Illinois Department of Financial and Professional Regulation. They weren't able to find Zach's license, but they encouraged me to file a complaint if I felt my situation warranted one and it would be looked into. I took a few days to think it through. Would it be the right thing to do? Maybe. But it bothered me that I had nothing concrete. Jackie said that he was dealing with some things and I didn't want to cause any harm or make things worse for him in case these reviews were the result of some malicious prank. On the other hand, I couldn't live with the thought that I may have been one in a long line of women he'd manipulated.

If the latter were the case, I wanted him to pay for the pain he'd caused me and any other patients he'd been involved with. I went back and forth for days, the decision eating away at me and consuming my every waking thought. Another week went by and still nothing. No other reviews, no evidence of his license being active or investigated, nothing.

There was just…nothing.

Chapter Fourteen

My hands were clammy and I wondered why I kept doing this to myself. Was I simply a glutton for punishment? As Jackie settled into her seat across from me, I couldn't help but think that was the only logical explanation. Just yesterday Anne and I were discussing what my options were. She was the one who suggested reaching out to Jackie again.

"Sit down and have a talk with her," she said, as if that was the easiest thing in the world to do and not a recipe for disaster. "At least that way it'll be confidential. Zach won't ever have to know and you may even get some answers."

It made sense. I *hated* that it made sense because that meant that I had no excuse not to call Jackie and request a meeting. I was surprised when she agreed to see me so soon. Her willingness made me wonder if maybe she knew why I was calling and was hoping to get some answers of her own. As it turned out, I wasn't too far off the mark. After telling her my concerns about the reviews I'd read and my relationship with Zach, she sagged in relief.

"I thought you might be her."

"Excuse me?"

She offered me a semblance of a smile. "I found out about you a while back," she explained. "Zach was telling me that he was in a relationship with someone. Someone he cared about deeply but that it was complicated since he was in a relationship." My heart did an odd little dance in my chest but I didn't interrupt. "Those reviews you read were actually written by his girlfriend's daughter. Apparently, the woman he's with now heard that he was seeing someone behind her back and her daughter lashed out."

This time it was my turn to sag in relief. So, that's what had happened. I was both relieved and angry. How could someone be that cruel to put something like that on the internet for all the world to see. She could have cost Zach his license and ruined his life. The irony that I was offended on his behalf after what had happened between us wasn't lost on me, but knowing that I wasn't a victim made my lingering loyalty to him an easier pill to swallow. Knowing that he wasn't some sort of monster, that there had at least been real feelings there, eased the weight off my shoulders. It did nothing to soften the hurt of being cut off so abruptly, but at least I hadn't fallen in love with a predator.

It wasn't much of a consolation, given the circumstances, but I'd take it. Jackie and I gossiped a little longer about Zach and the more she spoke, the more comforted I felt. She went on and on about how great he'd used to be and how lost he seemed now by comparison. Jackie was also kind enough to tell me how awful and crazy his new girlfriend was. Unsurprisingly, this news had the power to lift my spirits the most and I left Jackie's office feeling better than I had in weeks.

June rolled around and I met with Jackie for a second time, just to talk. It felt good to hash out what was happening with someone who knew both sides of the story and it allowed me to focus my burning curiosity about Zach in a way that didn't involve a search engine. Talking to Jackie made me feel somewhat OK. 'OK' as in I managed to go a few days without crying afterward and get out of bed when my alarm told me to come morning. For a little while, I didn't dwell on the situation that I was in – a much-needed respite from the heartbreak.

But the respite was only that, and all too soon I found myself struggling through the mire of depression that had been hounding me for so long. The loss of Zach made the sadness feel so much bigger, so much deeper, than before. As if I'd lost my footing and had fallen into a quagmire I had no hope of pulling myself from. Distractions lift the weight, if only for a moment. When I was investigating Zach I was able to trick myself into thinking that I was getting better. Now I knew the truth and had to occupy my mind in other ways. The only problem was that once the distraction was gone, I was back to fighting back tears several times a day.

Without meaning to, I found myself replaying conversations over and over again in my head, wondering if there had ever been anything real between us at all or if – like me – Zach had only been looking for a distraction from his own pain and unhappiness. I tried to convince myself that I would be OK. That there was a lesson in all of this and that sometimes there weren't any answers, but I couldn't accept that just yet. Even now, I questioned if there could be something worth fighting for between the two of us. But every time the thought crossed my mind, I wanted to punch myself in the face.

What the hell was the matter with me? Why was I still lingering in this purgatory of 'what if' and 'if only'? I felt so lost. So far removed from Chris that I doubted I could ever find my way back to him again. As much as I might want to feel the way that I used to towards him and as great as he was, those old emotions just weren't there anymore. Was it because I was still here, trapped in this limbo of emotion? Unable to pick one path over another? I couldn't shake the fear that the longer I lingered there the further Chris and I drifted mentally, physically, and emotionally from one another.

I was tired. Pain and confusion had been my reality for months now and some days, when the house was quiet and the vodka was a distant memory, I thought about just being done with it all. I was tired of being in pain and while I didn't take that next step and write a suicide note or plan how I wanted to go, the thought of making that pain stop grew into a fixation.

Life was about being happy, wasn't it? If I were going to keep living, I wanted to find happiness. Surviving from day to day this way was draining. The more run-down I felt, the greater the temptation to simply stop trying altogether grew. Sometimes I tried to shake it off, to tell myself to quit it with the pity-party and get over it already. But if therapy had taught me anything it was that my feelings were real, valid, and sometimes it seemed as if the bad ones wouldn't ever go away. I've read more self-help books than I can count, been to four different therapists almost weekly for the past three years, and yet I still wasn't OK. I was searching for answers and happiness like everyone else, and yet it seemed as if I was the only one who couldn't find them.

What wasn't I doing right?

How can I be happy? How do I learn to love life? Where was the recipe book? The game plan? What ingredients was I missing? I loved my kids. They were the one thing that felt right in this world. I loved spending time with them, watching them grow, teaching them, laughing at them and with them. The fact that I couldn't imagine a world without them was all that was keeping me going during those summer months. They were a constant reminder that I was lucky in so many ways. Still, I couldn't shake the knowledge that there was more to it. That there was more to life for me than always feeling as if I weren't good enough.

Like I said, I was tired.

Tired of feeling worthless.

Tired of feeling sad.

Tired of feeling anything at all.

***

Something had to give and I was afraid that if I didn't get some sort of closure, that it would be me. I spoke with Jackie and she agreed to help any way that she could. It took some convincing, but Zach finally agreed to meet with me as long as Jackie was there to play mediator. By the end of June, Jackie and I had mapped out how we wanted the meeting to go and what I wanted to accomplish by seeing Zach again. I was anxious to see him but terrified at the same time because I had no idea what to expect. It was like meeting a stranger. I didn't know if he would welcome the sight of me or be angry that I hadn't left well enough alone. Would he be cold and distant, or would he greet me as a friend? Which Zach would he give me? Which one did I want to see?

The week leading up to our meeting, I was too anxious to be sad. I only had one opportunity to say everything I needed to say and ask everything that had been on my mind these last few months. My biggest fear was that by the end of it all, I would still be left with unanswered questions. There was a part of me that questioned whether I should even see him; sometimes the loudest points are made by saying nothing at all. Only, I knew myself. If I didn't go, I would always wonder what would have happened, what he would have said and how he would have acted if I had. Zach had broken so many promises along with my heart and I knew that I needed this chapter of my life to come to a close before it could cause any more pain.

I needed to do this for myself.

That Thursday dawned cold and rainy, a gray start to what promised to be a gray sort of day. There was a somber feel to the air that made it feel as if I were on my way to a funeral. I was sad, anxious, and I cried the whole way there. Pulling into the parking lot, I wiped my tears and took a deep breath, trying to mentally prepare myself for what was about to happen.

As soon as I walked in I saw Zach and Jackie already waiting for me. At least I didn't have to drag this out any more than it needed to be, though having Zach's eyes on me as I moved across the room raised my anxiety to new heights. With Zach there, I barely even registered Jackie's presence. As soon as our eyes met, I found myself fixated on him. All the emotions I'd fought against since our breakup overwhelmed me. Shaky, I settled onto the couch across from them.

"Can we talk?" My gaze darted apologetically towards Jackie. "Alone, I mean?"

It didn't feel right to have a third party there and Zach must have felt the same, because he agreed. As Jackie stepped out, my eyes welled up and I fought to find the words I'd practiced in my head for so long.

"How could you?" I didn't mean for that to be the first thing that came out of my mouth, but it was my heart leading now instead of my head. As it turned out, I didn't have it in me for a carefully cultivated speech. "How could you just cut me off, without any warning, after leading me to believe that I would see you?" I shook my head and my voice broke. "I thought…" I couldn't finish the sentence but the words I'd left unsaid hung in the air regardless.

'I thought you cared about me?'

There was a flash of sincerity in his eyes, of raw emotion, that made me think that there had been something real between us after all. Maybe it had been just as hard for him to let me go as it had been for me. But I was tired of guessing and surmising. I needed to *know*. So I opened my mouth and told him everything. Everything that I had been holding back, things I'd been too afraid to admit even to myself about just how much he had meant to me and why. How the way that he'd left had nearly broken me. I opened my heart to him and, to my surprise, Zach returned the favor.

He spoke about missing me, about battling with himself and his own selfishness.

"I knew I should have let you go sooner, that I should have been honest, but I just couldn't bring myself to do it."

We talked for about an hour and in that time I spilled everything – everything that I had been aching to say for two years. The whole relationship. I questioned him, me, all of it. I felt so comforted to finally hear how he felt, and to be able to see and feel the emotion from him. Something that I hadn't gotten in so long. I'd begun to doubt that it had ever been there in the first place.

"I'm not sure how to leave you," I admitted as our conversation slowed and came to an end. It seemed cruel to make me walk away again.

"If you ever need anything you can still email me." He offered a small smile but his eyes were filled with something I liked to think may have been regret. "I meant it when I said that I want to be there for you."

I knew he shouldn't have done that, left the door slightly cracked that way, but I was relieved nonetheless. It brought me a measure of peace to know that he wasn't gone. Not completely. There was a knock on the door and I knew that it must be Jackie, signaling an end to Zach's and my time together. The two of us got to our feet and without thinking I stepped into his arms. It was the only real way to say goodbye. He held me close, his arms tight around me, and I clutched at him as if I could imprint this moment in my mind forever. I didn't want to let go and I knew he felt the same because as I tried to move away, he pulled me right back.

Just like always.

Watching him walk out the door and knowing that I would never see him again after today left me empty inside. I met his eyes again for the last time as he drove out of the parking lot and that was it. The last of us. I got in my car and the tears came in a torrent that I was sure would last forever.

Finally.

It was over.

Knowing that I'd finally found the closure I'd longed for for so long, the answers that I'd worked so hard for, should have been a relief.

And it was.

So why did the realization only make me cry that much harder?

***

Though the loss of Zach was still fresh in my mind and heart, I knew that it was time to focus on what remained of my relationship with Chris. Receiving the closure I'd longed for did not erase the months of pain or make the upcoming weeks any easier, but it was a step in the right direction. That's what I told myself when things grew too overwhelming. I was still drinking more than I should to cope and crying more than was probably healthy, but making the decision to confront Zach had galvanized me. It proved to me that I was stronger than I'd given myself credit for. For so long Zach had been the one person who made me feel whole, who understood me, and I'd faced him and had let him go.

Sometimes I still found myself hopeful that our paths would cross again. That Zach would someday be a part of my life again. I was probably making things more difficult for myself by believing that there was any chance of that, but sometimes when you feel something that strong and powerful you can't help but hope it will return. I wanted a happy ending, and in my wildest dreams that meant Zach finding his way back into my life again one way or another.

It's hard to comprehend having to mourn someone so important to me while he still exists. Our lives would always intersect, whether through conversation with mutual friends or through places that reminded me of him. I would probably run into him every now and again since we lived in the same area. It would be impossible to go through the rest of my life without being constantly reminded of this person who had played such an important role in my life and who had been such a staple in my mind and heart for the last two years.

There was no way to ever prepare yourself for losing someone you cared for so much, and there was no way the old Brianna would have been able to face Zach the way that I had knowing as much. It made me all too aware of what I needed to do next.

I'd been debating about whether or not to tell Chris about the affair and I knew I wouldn't be able to keep lying. Not to Chris or myself. Being with Zach and losing him had taught me so much about life. Mainly about what it meant to love and lose, and how no matter how much you experience both neither ever got any easier. My affair had hurt me more than I'd ever wanted to feel again and I had to keep reminding myself that I would be alright. I wasn't sure at first why Zach had been placed in my life or what I was supposed to learn from the experience, but I was determined to dedicate the next chapter of my life to finding out.

To doing better.

While I still felt strongly for Zach, there was no ignoring the guilt and pain that swamped me every time I thought of how all this would destroy Chris. I knew that I was inflicting the same pain onto him that Zach had me, and it was devastating.

At what point do you go with your heart over your head, or your head over your heart? Could logic lead me down the path of happiness and fulfillment or were the two mutually exclusive? Love used to make sense, Chris used to make sense, but now I recognized it for the easy route that it was and I was no longer sure I wanted to travel down that road.

I still wasn't sure what the right thing to do was or when I was supposed to stop fighting for us. What I did know is that I needed to move forward for myself, my husband, and even Zach. Both men had meant the world to me, but after experiencing something so real with Zach, I couldn't go back to the shadow my relationship with Chris had become. Even if I could move forward, Zach would always remain in my mind and in my heart. He would always be someone I would think about, wonder about, and Chris didn't deserve that.

It seemed silly, even ironic, that I was married to someone who adored me, who was loyal to me, and yet I was too distracted to acknowledge it. But then again, was I distracted or was it just that I had changed so much that I knew there was more that I wanted, that I needed, than that? I knew that I couldn't be the first person to experience these kinds of feelings. There had to be so many women out there who were in similar situations.

Even now, I try to throw logic at it as often as I can. Though in all honesty, I'm just feeling things out. Taking it all a step at a time and doing the best that I can along the way. I was tired of trying to drown my sorrows. I'd learned from watching my mother that there always seemed more to drown. At this point, the vodka has overstayed its welcome in my home. I still go to sleep – and sometimes wake up – crying, but that's going to be my reality for a while until the pain stops. I've come to accept that there are some things in life that I have no control over. Some things that I can't force or rush.

I have to focus on the things in life that I can control, and learn to forgive myself for those days when I don't have the strength to take a shower, let alone move from the comfort of my couch. I don't need to come up with a permanent solution, and every day I have to convince myself that there is light at the end of the tunnel and that the darkness that sometimes rears its ugly head will soon pass. Three years ago I couldn't imagine myself suffering anything remotely similar to the pain I've felt with this experience, yet here I was.

I was still going.

It's a struggle, and every day it takes everything in me to pull myself together: to go for a run, to take a shower, to put on some normal clothes. I'm not successful all the time, but I know that I have to keep trying. I'm so terrified of allowing myself to fall into the trap of forgetting that again. I think back to my mom and the pain she must have been suffering – the pain that led to her disease and eventually her death – and I think I'm stronger, more aware, because of her. I *want* to be stronger. I'd like to think that maybe that desire for better, that need to scale the mountain and reach the other side, is where half of the battle against the pain that once drove me is fought and – eventually – won.